Alive in Grace

Recipes for Vitality, Value, and Peace

Gabrielle Chavez

CoG Productions

Alive in Grace

© 2011 by Gabrielle Chavez

Cover design by Kathy Wu

Art by Dana Kelly Sweet

All text © 2011 COG Productions & Gabrielle Chavez

Graphics: George Mihaly
Photos: Andy Williams, Gabrielle Chavez

"The Triple Compass" reproduced by permission of DW Associates, LLC. Descriptions and reference to The Triple Compass as published in this book represent the interpretation, opinions & intent of the author Gabrielle Chavez and in no way reflect upon DW Associates, LLC.

NOTE TO READERS:
This book has been written and produced for informational purposes, should not be used as a substitution for consultation with health-care professionals. You should not consider educational material herein to be the practice of medicine or to replace consultation with a physician or other medical practitioner. The author is providing you with information in this work so that you can have the knowledge and can choose, at your own risk, to act on that knowledge. The author also urges all readers to be aware of their health status and to consult health care professionals before beginning any health program.

To the Christ the Healer UCC community members, past, present, and future

Contents

PREFACE

On Our Way Back Home

Every one of us born has already experienced bodily bliss, unity, oneness, wholeness, perfection—there are many names for this wonderful state of **Grace.**

Whatever conditions may have confronted us after birth, in the womb we were each bathed in warmth, fed, held, and protected from outside threat. We had no concern to support ourselves or even to know our "self" as separate.

Small wonder that a universal longing for a mythic "home" arises in we who have adapted to life outside of the womb, struggling to get along as individuals in an environment where our bodies are vulnerable and our minds become preoccupied with responding to our bodies' constant signals of hunger, thirst, heat, cold, pain, illness, and any number of threats to our comfort or survival.

Yet the memory persists that life could or should be better...*more*.

Most of us have experienced moments, even the briefest of moments, when that prenatal bliss returned—peak experiences, mystic in-breakings, being transported by art, music, nature, religious practices, or just spontaneous-seeming awakenings to universal awareness and love.

Can you imagine freedom, abundance, unity, joy, and peace? Can you envision yourself as embodied **Grace**? Imagine how that feels. What if you could do that now?

Seek And You Shall Find

One fascinating rabbi, named Jesus of Nazareth, declared that this "kingdom of heaven" was available in the *kairos* of now, in the moment.

No waiting, no lifetime of spiritual athleticism to win the prize.

His Jewish tradition identifies the kin-dom of heaven with *Shalom,* the return to the Garden of Eden, where God, humanity, and nature walk together in harmony.

For this Jesus invited his followers to pray, "That they all may be one, on earth as it is in heaven."

Today we call it the "kin-dom of heaven", as the word "kin" loses the imperial overtones of "king" and simply means one family.

Imagine a group of persons committed to exploring together what would happen if we actually trusted that the "kin-dom of heaven" was

among us

within us

now

near

as the prophet and rabbi Jesus proclaimed?

Since its inception, the experimental "Christ Curious" community we founded has been seeking this kin-dom of wholeness, or heaven.

We are passionate about finding the keys to the promised realm of **Grace** right here "on earth as it is in heaven."

We've learned a lot so far on our adventure.

Questing deeply along the path of Christ, we found pieces of a map and a compass, which we've put together and named as the **Compass of Grace** and the **Triple Compass Map**. Altogether we call our map and triple compasses the **Compass Way**.

Another treasure in our search for healing and wholeness has been the discovery of a healthy and joyful raw food lifestyle. While not required to attain states of embodied **Grace**, it sure helps us.

Thus this book, both an introduction to the **Compass Way** and also gourmet raw food. It comes out of the mesclun of food, spirituality, and community that has been our life since Christ the Healer UCC was birthed.

I am excited to share both the **Compass of Grace**—the center and goal of our **Compass Way** work—and also food whose natural goodness is not destroyed by cooking but whose taste is enhanced by human creativity. The **Compass of Grace** is the best recipe for a soul-centered embodiment I've found, so here's its story—served up with our latest, luscious, and lively-food recipes.

INTRODUCTION

Seeking the Kin-dom, Founding Christ the Healer

In October 1996 my beloved Thomas and I sent out 40 invitations to people we thought might be interested in co-creating "a new church, dedicated to the imitation of Christ both as assembler of community and practitioner of healing."

Twelve persons showed up for an initial gathering to compare notes on where, when, and how we each had sought and found heaven on earth. Inspired to continue our explorations at least weekly, we've been on an engrossing spiritual adventure in community ever since.

Many of us were not much, if at all, interested in Christianity, and most had explored a variety of other beliefs and practices. So we asked everyone who showed up, "What treasures have you found in your search for wholeness?

As a result, we together learned many healing modalities including Reiki, Body Electronics, sound healing, aroma therapy and flower essences; made drum circles, created labyrinths, meditated, sang and chanted in many languages, enjoyed ecstatic and Sufi dancing, wrote poetry, played with intuitive cards and games, shared writing and drawing from the soul, built a sweat lodge, explored esoteric Christianity, world religions, and mysticism, and eventually collected and circulated a 2000 volume library of spirituality and healing books.

As we engaged these practices, Thomas and I would find teaching moments to comment on how they dovetailed with Jesus' gospel of the kin-dom of heaven among us and open discussions on relevant biblical passages. In conversation with our mostly Christianity-averse folk, we slowly evolved a kind of "integrative Christianity," complementing the Western Christian tradition somewhat like what is now called "integrative medicine" expands and enhances the Western allopathic tradition.

Visionary socio-economic and political action in the footsteps of the revolutionary Jesus was always part of the mix. We attracted persons passionate about planetary as well as personal transformation, declared ourselves a peace church and sponsored many local peace actions, including a series of original and colorful "social exorcisms" and several public flag "washings."

The container we created to hold all this diversity was our model of "essential Christianity." By essential we mean the vital essence of the tradition as it speaks to most human hearts. With a congregation thirsty for the *experience* of healing or oneness—the kin-dom of heaven on earth--our contribution turns out to be complementing the rather intellectually-heavy Protestant tradition with embodied practices for essential Christianity that anyone can engage.

With Christ—the perfection of love on earth—at the center as our reference point, we created a circle that could be expanded as large as necessary to incorporate everyone without losing its shape.

Those of us who know, love, and are dedicated to Christ do our best to reflect and shine with the attractive light of Christ at the core.

Everyone is free to move closer to this light—or not—and still be included in the fullness of community.

Rather than try to convert or control people to a belief system through fear—which strikes me as profoundly unchristian—I simply aim to follow Christ and do what he said. Note that I said aim, not claim.

Our first members adapted this poem by Edwin Markham to describe our intention:

He drew a circle that cut me out
Heretic, rebel, a thing to flout
But Love and I conspired to win
We drew a circle that took him in

Our circle quickly took shape around a few defining principles:

Openness. As followers of Christ, we cannot imagine limiting questions, defending dogmas, or excluding anyone from anything.

Acceptance. Again, the reports in the Bible of the life and teachings of Jesus as he understood God weigh heavily towards non-judgment and freedom to learn from mistakes.

Spirit. Even if people are allergic to what they call "religion," most consider themselves "spiritual" as part of being human. Certainly we are more than current models of physicality and physics can measure. The terrain of spirit has been mapped by wise seekers over the eons and is available to anyone who wants it.

Further, Christ empowers his disciples with spiritual gifts such as healing and miracles; fruits—including love, joy, peace, and self-mastery—and guidance about "discerning the spirits."

Metanoia. A Greek word for expanding your mind, literally, "higher mind." Unhelpfully translated as "repent" in most English Bibles: "Repent, for the kingdom of God is near." Jesus is actually inviting us to raise our consciousness, not grovel, in order to find the kin-dom.

Practice. Because our bodies come with pre-loaded genetic software into the aforementioned threatening environment that shapes both our physical and psychological development, humans are unlikely to evolve beyond being small self-centered egos focused on survival and self-gratification without aspiration, effort, and community support. We are capable of learning more by choosing and re-choosing a loving and expanded life. See *Metanoia.* Practice does make a difference.

Embodiment. This vital principle has two essential meanings:

> 1) You have a body. This is good. Don't just live in your head. Rejoice in being here and having all the experiences of physical life, come what may.

> 2) Though we each have a unique and particular perspective, we are part of a larger whole, not isolated individuals. This means we will find fulfillment in aggregate, like individual organs finding their place as members of a body.

Sacrifice. Another scary word that deserves better. It means literally, "to make sacred." Sacrifice is the deepest and most transformational insight of essential Christianity. It involves giving "up," not as loss, but as liberation. Persons who practice the magic of self-sacrifice are fearless, powerful, and radically content.

Help. All kinds of it: the help from fellow humans we know, and so many others whose striving creates fields of possibilities and patterns that inspire and support our aspiration and effort. Our inner guidance, as we learn to discern and trust it. And for those who choose to align with Christ, a powerful, perfected pattern of human potential to follow, a master and friend to commune with and call upon in need.

Over the years, through many adventures and folks coming and going, we became a recognized congregation of the United Church of Christ denomination.

The roots of the UCC incorporate four streams of Protestant Christianity, both old world and new. Because the denomination grew from separated churches seeking common communion, it carries the energy and intention of aggregating, not splitting, as so many religious groups experience, and thus remains committed to diversity, not creedal lock step and enforcement of doctrine.

At its best, the United Church of Christ is a "walk together" church, meaning individual congregations agree voluntarily to associate or "walk together" in their journey of faith to create a denomination.

I love the acronym for UCC my mother coined: **U C**an **C**hange!

There is no bishop, pope, or hierarchical authority over any UCC churches. They are democratic organizations of members. Numbering a little more than a million souls, the United Church of Christ isn't as large or well-known as many other denominations and churches, so this information may bust stereotypes some folks have about Christians.

Christ the Healer was welcomed into the UCC family to give its gift without being told how to "do church." I have been grateful for the freedom to explore as well as the deep roots in Christian faith and wider connection the UCC provides.

Eating and Healing

When we heard that the gospel of Jesus could be summarized as "eating together and healing," we at Christ the Healer decided to be an "eating together and healing church."

Every one of our (mostly evening) gatherings, where we explored healing in community, included the sharing of food. People participated enthusiastically, and CtH came to have the most interesting potlucks and "coffee hour" of any church I've known.

Two of the many healing modalities we explored immediately took root in the soil of our community and continue to flourish there today. One is Reiki, an energy healing technique created in Japan by Mikao Usui in the early 20th century.

Beautifully simple, accessible to all ages and conditions, Reiki allows most people to actually feel (often for the first time) a flow of energy that is deeply peaceful and refreshing after a short class and attunement. A gift from Eastern spirituality, Reiki is easily translatable into other spiritualities, including Christianity. Christ the Healer UCC has made a mission of teaching Reiki to churches wishing to create hands on healing prayer groups. A paper I published, "Reiki for Christians," is available on our website: **http://cthgathering.org/reiki/**

The other major practice we adapted and adopted is called "Body Electronics" (BE).

BE is such a powerful, embodied expression of our central principles that it quickly became a core practice offered to members and friends of Christ the Healer UCC. Practiced successfully, BE is a high-demand, high-commitment undertaking, yet we have never lacked for takers in our ongoing weekly group.

Thoroughly holistic, Body Electronics is a group practice that engages the spirit, emotions, mind, and body. It involves

   --a commitment to supporting others,
   --facing and embracing one's mental and emotional resistances with love,
   --preparing the body nutritionally to physically benefit from the regenerative
     energy that circulates in a "point holding" table session.

For more information on Body Electronics, read *Body Electronics—Vital Steps to Physical Regeneration* by Thomas C. Chavez or go to our website, **www.cthgathering.org**.

www.amazon.com/Body-Electronics-Vital-Physical-Regeneration/dp/1556435177

Raw Food Comes to Dinner at Christ the Healer

Nutritional preparation for a Body Electronics point holding session includes saturating the body with trace minerals and enzymes, which are largely missing from the Standard American Diet.

Though the founder of Body Electronics, John Whitman Ray, recommended eating a diet at least 70% raw food for best healing results, in the beginning most of us found food enzymes taken with meals to be an acceptable substitute for the radical discipline of adopting a diet consisting mostly of uncooked fruits, nuts and vegetables.

Except for Jim, a tall skinny quiet guy with long hair who looked like Jesus in the pictures. I noticed Jim always brought big delicious salads to share at our potlucks and then I discovered that he ate raw food *all* the time.

Somewhat horrified, yet wanting to demonstrate care for him, I began bringing a dish of fresh fruit or vegetables along with my cooked creations to our gatherings.

Jim never really talked about his food choices, but did invite us to a raw food festival that was held in Portland, Oregon that year, in 2000. Curious to learn about what Jim treasured, I and a few others attended.

Many of the raw foodists I saw impressed me with their vitality and energy. The food was pretty good, too, and a lot of the speakers made a compelling case for their diet.

Because of that experience, Thomas bought me a raw "un-cook" book. We made a few new dishes for our potlucks but otherwise didn't change our eating patterns as it seemed too demanding.

The next year we went to the festival as vendors in the Healing Arts area, offering some of the energy work we had learned to do, including Reiki.

Igor Boutenko of the "Raw Family" was so impressed with his Reiki attunement and some healing Thomas helped facilitate that he sent over platters of their gourmet raw food to our booth three times a day for the duration of the festival.

Between that and listening to a presentation by Victoria Boutenko, we were hooked, and plunged into a 100% raw food lifestyle that very day.

I do not recommend this drastic and sudden a change unless you are ready, willing, and able to make it work. We were.

For us, it involved a steep re-learning curve both in how to eat and how to prepare the food. We experimented so enthusiastically that I had learned enough to write a whole book by 2005, *The Raw Food Gourmet, Going Raw for Total-Well-Being.*

http://www.amazon.com/Raw-Food-Gourmet-Going-Well-Being/dp/1556436130

Thomas and I quickly realized that we would have to develop community support for our new lifestyle, as eating is a communal act. Potlucks at Christ the Healer began to change.

I could write another book about how challenging it is to share your passion, enthusiasm, and recipes for a new way of eating with others in your community who haven't been similarly inspired. Many reacted defensively even though I felt I was bending over backwards to be as accepting of what others eat as their religious beliefs.

I have always insisted that for me, raw food is not a religion (though after hanging out with some raw foodists, one might wonder) but a spiritual practice.

As I began eating this way, I felt better and got more out of my Body Electronics sessions. The energy of youth returned and little nagging chronic things like dandruff, post nasal drip, constipation, frequent colds and sore throats just went away. At first my weight plummeted, then re-normalized as a fit and trim size 8.

My palate came alive, and I began to appreciate and enjoy flavors as never before. Our garden grew and carbon footprint shrank as we were drawn to eat higher quality and fresher local produce.

Best of all, my experience of energy and spirit expanded in gratifying ways and I felt more connected to nature.

Disorganized Religion

By design, Christ the Healer UCC has always taken shape around the gifts and passions of its members. Lacking a rigid structure, our congregation is somewhat like an amoeba, flowing along, putting out a pod in the direction where the energy is flowing. Thus we have been known over the years as a drumming church, a Reiki church, a Body Electronics church, and a radical peace church due to the output of members' activism.

Now we were being called a "raw food church."

Believe me, this did not increase our popularity back in 2001. At that time, embracing a raw vegan lifestyle was about the most counter-cultural thing you could do, inside or outside of Christianity. It affected our daily lives in a way that put us completely opposite the prevailing culture.

Though I knew I had just made my greatest transformation in a lifetime of spiritual aspiration and growth, I did not consider how personally challenging and off-putting it would be not only for church members, but also colleagues, friends and family to feel welcome and accepted at table with me.

We had been companions, yet my daily bread had changed. People felt uncomfortable, and many distanced themselves.

Let's just get this out of the way: I neither demand that Christians become raw-foodists, nor that raw foodists become Christians. Eating raw is not my religion. Nor do I subscribe to raw food dogmas any more than to Christian dogmas.

There is information, and there is choice. For me, both are constantly changing. Here I simply invite you to taste and see the treasures I've found.

As we changed, Christ the Healer began to attract new folk. Younger people experimenting with a raw food lifestyle began to show up, bringing their dishes to our gatherings. We started hosting raw food potlucks as well as continuing our regular potluck. These became so popular that eventually we held a "raw curious" potluck each week in a different part of the Portland metro area.

We catered parties and events with raw gourmet food and trained young chefs in a new weekly Sunday Supper gathering, launching a few careers and making lots of new friends.

SUNDAY SUPPER
WELCOME

PROVIDED BY:

CHRIST THE HEALER
UNITED CHURCH OF CHRIST

By 2006, we had built enough of a raw-friendly community to sponsor Christ the Healer's first Raw and Living Spirit Retreat at the Central Pacific Conference UCC's Camp Adams south of Portland.

It is three nights and four days featuring the product of our best efforts to find and access the kin-dom of heaven, Christ the Healer's **Compass of Grace** and the **Compass Way**. (More about these soon!) Not to mention a smörgåsbord of gourmet raw food at every meal!

www.rawandlivingspirit.org

Food as Communion

The Holy Communion liturgy I grew up with in church includes this prayer from the book of Isaiah describing the great in-gathering of the tribes at the dawn of the long-promised return of Eden.

> *They shall come from the east and the west, from the north and the south,*
> *to sit at table in the kingdom of heaven.*

When the Bible pictures the peaceable kingdom with humans in it, it is not a tableau of lion and lamb, predator and prey nestled together in the wild, but a domestic scenario of all peoples sitting down at the table, feasting in peace. The heavenly banquet is such a beautiful, earthy metaphor for the embodiment of **Grace.**

Consider eating—a necessary, mostly daily, activity of being human in body; a visceral reminder of our connection to the rest of nature; a miraculous alchemical transformation of foodstuffs into the elements for our body's growth, function, and repair.

Then consider the long journey our food takes to arrive on our plates, the times of planting and harvesting, the many hands it passes through including, finally, those in the kitchen.

Few, if any of us, can produce all the food we eat without other humans. None can produce food without the cooperation of nature, even the most chemically altered formulations.

So the simple act of eating connects us intimately on many levels with each other as well as the natural world we are part of. Mindful of this, eating becomes a sacrament of oneness.

Jesus also set apart the meal time as a sacred moment, an *anamnesis,* or present reminder, of the truth of our wholeness.

Like a hologram, there is one bread but many pieces, one body with many parts sharing the same life. "Every time you eat and drink," he told his followers at supper, "Remember what I have taught you."

His teachings are quite easy to remember; in a word, **"Love."** In a few more words, **"Share. Serve. Trust. Give. Rejoice. Forgive."**

Jesus understood profoundly what science now tells us: we are all one body, composed of endlessly recycled shared molecules.

His passionate gospel rings more urgently than ever today: the kin-dom of heaven, the oneness of all creation in harmony and peace, *is near, within us, and among us.*

The Compass of Grace

The **Compass of Grace** is our name for the practice we refined and developed in the Christ the Healer community over years of walking together (and sometimes wandering around) seeking the kin-dom of heaven on earth.

The **Compass of Grace** is the jewel of the **Compass Way**, which provides a map of where we are coming from in our relationships and a means (or compass) to reorient ourselves to a state of **Grace.**

Together the **Compass of Grace** and the **Compass Way** amount to a stunning breakthrough that can clarify and uplift human relations for anyone who seeks to understand and improve them.

We've been practicing it these last few years and are gratified to see its growing effect in our lives and community.

Now, in this book, we offer you our simple new synthesis of ancient and modern wisdom that is easy to understand and apply to daily life.

Acknowledgments

Incorporated into the **Compass Way** are many of the principles of Body Electronics, itself a distillation of highly effective holistic knowledge.

We are deeply indebted to all the teachers that passed through our lives and community offering wisdom and transformational practices which we shared among ourselves and adapted.

Whatever spiritual treasures anyone brought into our circle we explored, from *A Course in Miracles* to the Work of Byron Katie.

We were inspired by more of these than we can name, but a short list of major influences would include John Ray, the founder of Body Electronics, and Victoria Boutenko of the Raw Family, who combines **Grace** with living foods better than anyone we know. More inspiration came from our studies with Warren Wolf, who gave us names and demonstrations for the connection between psychological states and physical tension, and Dr. Richard Bartlett, whose teaching goes beyond healing that you can explain through process into what he calls quantum shifts, or discontinuities, that allow anything to happen.

Theological teachers who were instrumental in my understanding of the social implications of transformational healing include Walter Wink, Miraslov Wolf, most especially my father Gabriel Fackre, and behind him, Jesus.

Jesus was the first person to teach me that I could choose to "seek first the kin-dom of heaven" and then earthly problems would sort themselves out. In whatever else I learned from other teachers, my heart always asked, just how does this help me follow Christ towards "on earth as it is in heaven?"

To embody the **Grace** of Christ on this planet is my personal quest, which for me must be beyond teaching and preaching the words to living them.

I am love
I am loving
I love
I am

I am love in the body
I am loving in the body
I love the body
I am the body

I am love in the body of Christ
I am loving in the body of Christ
I love the body of Christ
I am the body of Christ

--from the CtH Notebook of Words

Lost and Found

The search for **Grace,** for the kin-dom of heaven on earth, grows from the pain of paradise lost. To put it in modern terms, you could say our human operating system is in a bind and needs an upgrade.

The bind, of course, is that ancient split between our higher human potential and aspiration (often called the soul) and our limited personality identified with our body-mind—the "bind" that limits our realization of the gracious one-ness we know is our truth.

Though most of us unquestioningly identify with our personality, also known as "small self," unmasked it is merely a bundle of habitual emotional reactivities and resistances.

At its best, our personality functions like a clever and well intentioned politician to help us "get along" in life. At its worst, it convinces us to pour our life force into an arms race of self-defense and pre-emptive aggression, ultimately creating a hell on earth in our own psychology as well as in relationships with fellow humans caught in the same bind.

Unlike other animals that we know of, the human mind evaluates and elaborates our physical and emotional sensations. When something happens to us, we think about it. We talk about it. We compare it to memories of what we've already experienced. Our brains create associated neurophysiology and neurochemistry.

The ability to think, to access a memory or feel an emotion is a use of our creative imagination. We do this so naturally it seems very "real."

The strong mind-body connection we have means that our memories, thoughts and emotions—all of which are the product of our imagination, are affecting our physiology all the time.

Our imaginations can work for us or against us.

For example, remember something unpleasant or unhappy. Notice how your state of being changes when you do. Changes in posture, voice, breathing, perspiration, muscle tension, facial expression, skin temperature, heart rate and many other physical effects ensue when we use the power of our imagination to bring an emotionally charged memory to mind.

If you keep this up, you will override your immune responses enough to induce symptoms and even make yourself sick. As a child, I discovered how to create credibly inflamed eyes, ears, and throat to avoid going to school when I didn't want to, just by imagining how sick I could be.

OK, stop the movie if you've gotten the point. Take a breath, shake yourself out, and congratulate yourself on your powerful mastery of mind over matter.

Now use the same mastery to gently bless your memory and release it.

Our bodies actually "hold" our memories for us, which is what gives such surprising power to the choice to reanimate them. We can even enhance this ability to re-experience a full body memory by fantasizing, elaborating the story of the original event or trigger until it reaches a pleasurable or painful emotional and physical peak.

Isn't this what others do who are masters at manipulating our emotional responses? Advertisers, filmmakers, novelists, political speakers, talk show hosts, friends, children, lovers?

If you develop the discipline to create a meta-position of awareness from which you can stand back and track the ceaseless flow of your own thoughts and emotional responses, you will notice that left to its own devices, the mind wanders all over the place, leaving you to react robotically to whatever sensations, feelings, or suggestions come into your field, many of them unconscious.

Learning how to meditate, to relax into a stillness of body, emotion, and mind, allows us to simply observe and not always react to all the passing internal thoughts and streaming sensations. One consciousness researcher has coined the metaphor, "cortical-thalamic pause" to describe the exercise of stopping the flow before it carries us away.

In order to keep from being lost in the seas of mindless reactivity and auto-pilot run amok mental ping-ponging, it is most helpful to have a map of the places your imagination might take you, and a well-honed practice of entering into chosen states of higher consciousness.

We offer ours here.

A Map and a Compass

There are many maps and many ways to describe the same territory. Jesus used a beautifully simple one, whose descriptions we have updated.

Essentially, you might find yourself operating in one of three different states of being, which he referred to as heaven, earth, (or "this world") and hell.

We call these the realms of **Grace, Getting Along,** and **Self Protection.**

Earth is where our soft fleshy bodies are born, where they struggle to survive, and inevitably die.

Born, we quickly forget oneness, and find ourselves shockingly, apparently alone, subject to overwhelming, uncontrollable feelings and sensations, dependent upon others to survive.

To manage successfully in our vulnerable bodies in "this world" —another name Jesus used—we discover ways to "get along" in the conditions we confront. The strategies we develop to solve the problem of life on earth vary.

Some of us are more successful than others. There are winners and losers in the struggle for physical and psychological comfort.

Of course, everyone loses the game of life at death, but that doesn't stop most of us from trying to get what we want and hold on to it as long as possible.

Whatever else you may believe about it, hell is a state of mind, which we may visit often during our lifetime, and one most of us know all too well. Essentially "hell," as we are speaking of it, is the realm of **Self Protection** where we retreat when our efforts to **Get Along** in this world fail to satisfy.

To protect myself from perceived pain, attack, loss, failure, or disappointment, I might use my imagination to further the illusion of separation by creating enemies, avoiding, defending, attacking, isolating, annihilating—all the strategies that lead to being at war with others, self, life.

By adulthood, I am probably so good at this that my self-protective reactions are so automatic they seem natural and obvious. Many, indeed, are culturally reinforced.

Think of most pop and country music lyrics. Who doesn't blame you if you reject someone who's "done you wrong?"

The states of "earth" and "hell" or, "hell on earth," are the realm of duality—functioning in the unquestioned belief in the separate small self or personality and its perceived experiences.

In **Getting Along,** we attempt to engage connection with others from a point of view of separation. When we aren't **Getting Along** and drop into a state of **Self Protection**, our posture and behavior disengage connection—also from a presumption of separativeness.

Finding our Bliss

Counter to the culture of separation is the kin-dom of heaven, or state of **Grace**—shalom, wholeness, oneness, non-duality and non-separation—many names describe it. We may experience it as a state of consciousness like the higher mind of *metanoia* mentioned earlier.

For purposes of mapping this state, we give it eight landmarks or entry points, creating what we call a "**Compass of Grace**". The eight entry points are: **Acceptance, Gratitude, Joy, Inspiration, Awe, Peace, Presence, Love**.

These words are quite familiar from Biblical tradition and in general use. In our workshops, we use the familiarity both to trigger body memories and to facilitate remembering.

Though the words are familiar in many contexts, we are using them in a very specific sense in the **Compass**. Each of these named states of **Grace** is *unconditional* and always available to everyone. (Please be aware that if you are or have been a Roman Catholic, the phrase "state of grace" may mean something quite different than what we are saying here.)

Grace is not dependent on outside conditions, but received from within. Thus in a state of **Grace**, one may have no reason to feel **Gratitude,** but it is present. Less than no reason to be in **Love**, yet one simply is. One is "Surprised by **Joy**," and finds "**Peace** that passes understanding."

Grace is unity—indivisible--so all these named states of **Grace** inter-penetrate. Identifying yourself in one state of **Grace** gives you access to the whole **Compass.** If you are in **Joy**, you have instant access to **Peace, Love, Inspiration,** etc.

Many of us who have been blessed with blissful experiences find ourselves transported in them away from our ordinary lives, and even bodily awareness. Lots of religious practices and even some chemicals can facilitate experiences of transcendence into unitive awareness.

Unfortunately, the ecstatic moment passes, the workshop high ends, the drug wears off, and the demands of "real life" intrude, taking us back to the struggles of this world until the next opportunity to tune in and drop out presents itself.

Our only consolation might be to focus upon an afterlife heaven, where the cares that come with having a body in this world finally fall away.

But here's the great news: one of Jesus' remarkable innovations was to challenge his followers to imagine that they could create a fourth state, heaven on earth, by being "in the world, but not of it." We are calling this fourth state "**Embodied Grace.**"

The Triple Compass

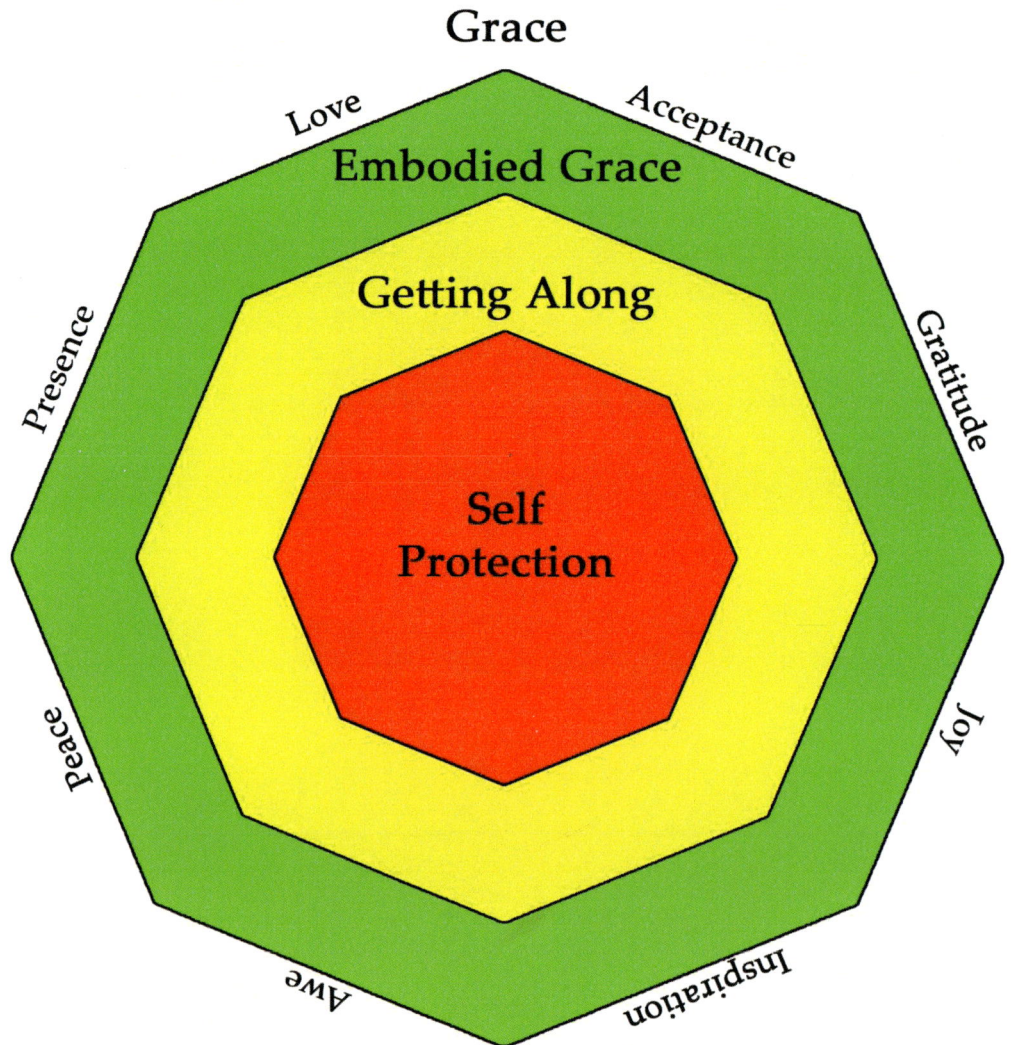

Grace

Love

Acceptance

Embodied Grace

Presence

Gratitude

Getting Along

Self
Protection

Peace

Joy

Awe

Inspiration

Embodied Grace is something we can aspire to and choose to practice. Our intention is to access the kin-dom of heaven here and now as Jesus promised.

That means feeling and being the presence of **Grace** where we live. It is the longed for "upgrade" of our human operating systems!

Studying the gospel reports of Jesus' life and teachings with this in mind can be quite illuminating. Notice how Jesus, at one with God and inspired by the Spirit, effects dramatic physical release with a look, a touch, a breath, a word of command.

From the place of oneness, he demonstrated more power to affect *this world* than any civil or religious power or demon ever has.

Is Jesus the only one who can do this? Did he come just to show off? These same accounts of his miracles constantly tell how he instructed, empowered and commanded his followers to do likewise.

Besides his powerful demonstrations, Jesus passionately preached, prayed, and occasionally lost his temper to persuade the willfully blind and ignorant that the kin-dom of heaven, the realm of God, belongs right here on earth.

> *Our Father in Heaven,*
> *hallowed be your name.*
> *Your kingdom come,*
> *your will be done,*
> *on earth as it is in heaven.*
> *--Matthew 6:9-10*

John Dominic Crossan, a respected New Testament scholar, has come to this stunning conclusion from his studies of the gospels: ***"The kingdom of heaven is the only way that works."***

I don't believe this is a dogmatic statement, but a matter of fact observation.

If humans trusted the original truth of oneness, everyone would feel safe on earth, even in bodies, for we would each hold and care for all others as aspects of our own self.

This would work in much the same way as a healthy body operates as a whole, individual parts cooperating to maintain health and function.

All of that struggle to survive individually would become the effort of our collective genius to create the conditions of health and sanity on our beautiful and abundantly provisioned planet.

We know this. We can already imagine how to get there from here. There are thousands of great teachers, blueprints, websites, and small model communities with viable programs.

What stops us but the failure of will to embody our truth—and the prospect of losing what we presently hold fast as our reality?

What stops us dead is that in this world as presently constructed, anyone who tries to live with full faith in the kin-dom of God is swimming so upstream against the tide of culture that they are likely to pay the price Jesus quoted and paid himself: "Whoever wants to save their life must lose it."

This invitation to sacrifice sets off all the alarm bells in our genetically and culturally conditioned systems. Who wants to let go of everything they currently know and count on, throw caution to the winds, trust the promise of abundant life and follow Christ's example?

Maybe St. Francis and St. Clare and a few others. But it's going to take a lot of heroes to reach the tipping point where the entrenched ways of this world yield to the greater power of **Grace** and make the water safe for the timid.

Who wants to be first?

It is, as Jesus once observed, especially difficult for a "rich man"—rich, as so many of us are just by living in the materialistic first world—to enter the kin-dom of heaven. Those who have less to lose might have an easier time making the leap. Or, conversely, they might be so downtrodden and encased in **Self Protection** against overwhelming conditions that they never unfold into the light of the kin-dom among us either.

So most of us choose to work on our own private kingdoms, settling for what comforts and pleasures we can get instead of **Joy**, relations which are transactions instead of unconditional **Love**, living mentally in the past or future instead of fully **Present**, slaves to the streams of our own unconscious and the manipulations of more powerful others.

Looked at this way, we humans have made a poor bargain by believing the dualistic dogma of the "prince of this world," the archetypal devil.

The kin-dom of heaven is the only way that works because **Love** is the foundation of this world.

It is how we were designed to function—*in this world*.

You can prove this to yourself by using your imagination to recall a time when you experienced one of the points on the **Compass of Grace**. Bring the scene of that remembered **Joy, Peace, Awe, Gratitude**, etc., forward and notice all the details with a movie director's eye.

Be there now.

>Experience your past state of **Grace** as a full-bodied memory.

Now make it more wonderful, loving, joyous. Intensify that exalted feeling.

As you get into it, use your capacity to observe yourself from a meta-position of awareness to track your responses. Notice any shifts in your state of being— breathing, posture, muscle tension—how you are holding yourself.

Do you feel better? Is your posture more relaxed and open? Does it feel "right", even "natural", the way things are supposed to be?

When we do this exercise in a group, the experience is particularly powerful, because humans unconsciously resonate and enhance each other's thoughts and feelings like a soaring flock of birds (or a mob of panicked lemmings.)

Even the tenor of the room seems to change. Many feel a stillness, peace, harmony—sacred space—that they had not noticed moments previously.

Do you want to feel this way all the time? Do you long for a better world? Your yearning is a prayer, the compass arrow pointing to **Grace.**

Consciousness Technology

What if you could be in **Grace** as a steady state—doing the dishes, driving a car, sitting at a desk, standing in line, facing illness, interacting with others? If you engaged the previous exercise of your imagination, notice how easy it was to experience a difference in the moment simply by choosing to shift your attention.

Will, attention, and imagination are human characteristics that we are free to develop.

Undeveloped, we become less and less free as stronger currents in our environment influence how our will, attention, and imagination are employed.

Many of those stronger currents may be our own unconscious patterning, robotically driving our emotional reactions, life experiences, and perceptions.

Just as muscle memory develops through practice, making it unnecessary to think how to drive a car once you have learned, it has been shown that our brains change in response to our habitual thought patterns and emotions. The circuitry in a person's brain who becomes chronically depressed shows up differently on a brain scan from what it was previously.

On the other hand, we can practice states of **Grace** and develop brains which support higher consciousness as our normal state—*change your mind and change your brain.*

As long as we are conscious, humans are free to choose. We are free to choose how we exercise our consciousness. Where we put our attention. Whether we are willing to notice and take charge of our streaming emotional reactivity. How we judge our perceived experiences.

Interestingly, the amount of incoming sensory data and detail we can consciously notice or "think about" in any given moment is minuscule compared to what our machines can track. Recorders and scanners pick up all kinds of information we miss about events we witness. And even within the tiny bandwidth of data we can potentially name and notice, fellow humans sharing the same experience will often have radically different reports.

So what we decide to tell ourselves (and others) about what is real is both selective and a choice. Someone once calculated that of the billions of bits of sensory information coming into our field each second, we can at best consciously notice or recall no more than fourteen.

One of the ways to navigate in the sea of information is to take those few bits of experience we've noticed and use our imagination to create a story that "makes sense" of them. My husband Thomas compares this to selecting beads to string together for a necklace.

Then we have an imaginative creation we can compare with others' made up stories of their perceived experience.

Most of us don't feel comfortable being around people whose stories of reality are drastically different from our own. We may try to change them by telling them our story. They may try to change us.

On the other hand, we *could* choose to enlarge our perspective on reality by incorporating the other's point of view. After all, we are capable of noticing how little we notice.

We can decide to embrace others with their stories to expand our appreciation of life.

When humans agree to imagine together, creativity is unleashed and new "things" are discovered. Powerful good can come from collaboration and appreciation of the diverse gifts and perspectives of others.

This is the working principle of the "Body of Christ" where each one is treasured for their essential uniqueness in a field of harmonic agreement, also known as the "Mind of Christ".

If we do not welcome the discomfort of bumping up against a story of reality that radically challenges our own, however, this can lead to impassioned arguments, fighting, and eventually, war.

As we see on our **Triple Compass Map**, defending and attacking amount to the same thing, i.e., choosing to imagine we are separate and alone, fighting for our lives in the veritable "hell on earth" of the **Self Protection Compass.**

U Can Change

Though it took me some time to believe it, it now seems obvious to me that where I focus my attention and imagination—and therefore what I experience as reality—is an act of will.

Therefore, I can choose where I am standing on the map of heaven, embodied **Grace**, earth, and hell.

And I can choose, and re-choose.

To remain in embodied **Grace** I have to exercise choice, because the very condition of perceiving myself here in a body (the alternative is a deal-breaker) sets some limits to my perceived "reality."

For one, it puts me into the consensus reality of untold generations of human story-telling about the trials and tribulations of embodiment, a powerful consciousness field defining the "rules of the game" for each human born into it.

> "Finitude," the theologians call it. All who are born, die.

So unless I choose to become disembodied, either ultimately or temporarily by interfering with my biochemistry—or more commonly, simply by living in my head—I need to develop strategies to be graciously "in the world and not of it".

The strategy that we have found works best is to use the **Triple Compass Map** to locate where we are functioning at the moment. Simply check in with yourself and ask.

Self-awareness is the beginning of freedom to choose. It is obvious to any sincere questioner, and certainly to anyone around us, whether we are coming from **Grace**, this world's concerns of **Getting Along**, or the realm of **Self Protection.** Our posture, stance, voice, and face all broadcast our state of consciousness.

Notice, for instance, where your consciousness is focused now. Are you delighted? Expanded? Joyous? Full of open-hearted compassion for yourself and all your relations? Is there mind chatter going on in the background as you read? What is it saying? Are you thinking about the past or future?

If you are in worry or regret, you are not present in **Grace,** but most likely stressing over how to "**Get Along**" better in some way. Notice how you are holding yourself. Can you change that?

If you are mentally arguing or defending yourself from someone or something or hunkering down behind a psychic wall (enumerating the reasons and justifications for it), you are actually at war with your life and functioning in the **Compass of Self Protection**. How does that feel?

Once you have located yourself, notice how your body is out-picturing your state of consciousness in posture, breathing, muscle tension, temperature, and anything else you can become aware of physically. Just notice, and remember.

We have learned that embodied states of **Grace** correlate with relaxation, postural alignment, unhindered breathing, strong circulation, and a felt sense of overall well-being in the body.

Conversely, stressing over how to **Get Along** and engaging in the various forms of **Self Protection** looks and feels like physical contraction, constricted breathing and circulation, and postural distortions. The whole arena of mind-body medicine confirms these observations.

These physical distortions are more evidence that "the kin-dom of heaven is the only way that works."

Grace is our natural state, what our friend Philip Morgan, who has been thinking about these things with us, calls a "co-present parallel reality" when seen from the perspective of non-states of **Grace.**

Now that you have this data from your own bio-feedback, consider your choices.

You may choose to engage your skills and resources to work harder or work smarter to succeed in whatever you hold to be important in this world. To **Get Along** better.

You may indeed, through this effort, have the satisfaction of being at least a partial "winner" in the game of life. There are definitely winners and losers all around us in this world. At least until death when even the winners lose all.

Alternately, you may decide that "life is hell" and focus on all the evidence you have to prove it, creating even more proof by triggering unpleasant reactions in those around you as you enhance your aura of negativity and elaborate your painful stories.

You will mostly likely be very successful at this. So successful, that digging out of it if you decide you want something else seems impossible.

Usually, we bounce between these first two realms most of the time, reserving **Self Protection** for certain failed relationships and situations while continuing the uphill struggle to mostly **Get Along**.

Or we may choose to trust in a benign universe loving enough to cast our cares upon and hold us even as we were held in the womb; choose to access this state of remembered and yearned-for **Peace**, satisfaction and wholeness. Choose **Grace,** whatever the "facts on the ground" we may be noticing at the time.

You can even choose **Grace** from the deepest pit of despair—but only if you are willing to surrender your pride, your story, and how you hold reality *completely*.

This choice can be quite dramatic. Finding yourself in hell, you can hit the bottom, fall through, and discover the exciting but messy "shipwreck, gladness, and amazement" route to salvation.

Various spiritual exercises recommended in the coming chapters and certain (not recommended) chemical substances can also "up the odds" of reaching a mystical state of transcendence.

Embodied Grace

However you get there, your bliss will either be a (necessarily limited) out of body experience or an exalted state of consciousness that you learn to inhabit in your daily life. This latter is the human capability we are calling "embodied **Grace**."

I am not knocking peak experiences, spiritual highs, and out of body transcendence states. They show what is possible and make wonderful vacations. But I want to bring them home to where I live. Don't you?

The beauty of choosing embodied **Grace** is you will no longer experience yourself as separate and alone. That in itself is a portion of heaven, a release from the heavy burdens of life.

In a state of **Grace**, you are in harmony, in *shalom* with all that is. Support shows up in the form of serendipities, synchronicities, coincidences, miracles, and angels in disguise or otherwise.

Life, *your life,* gets interesting and wonderful as you "repent" or change your consciousness to the meta state of **Grace.**

With practice, the state of embodied **Grace** becomes both more spontaneously present and also more available when you really need it. This is the process of being "filled with the Holy Spirit," or *sanctification,* supposed to arise in Christian experience from being "born again" or "born from above."

Saints, at least in the Christian tradition, are recognized as much for their positive impact on this world as their mystical attainments. They go about their often very ordinary lives in this world graced with a radiant spiritual presence that uplifts everyone around them.

Spiritual writer Carolyn Myss has coined the phrase, "mystics without monasteries" to challenge those of us today who seek to carry the **Grace** experienced in the stillness of meditation, contemplation, and prayer into the world without a monastic community to relieve us of worldly concerns.

Quantum Saintliness

For years studying the Catholic saints, I have pondered the conundrum that although tremendous effort and spiritual striving characterize most of their lives to a greater or lesser degree, those who appear to radiate the greatest blessing do so naturally and effortlessly, as though they had broken through into a reality—a level of consciousness—where there is no striving, no process, just simply being.

From the other end, Protestant Christians parse the same conundrum called "salvation by faith" versus "salvation by works" as we struggle to accept God's undeserved love and **Grace** while fighting our own perfectionistic psychology that desperately believes we need to do something to be saved.

It seems that you cannot "take the kin-dom of heaven by a storm" of spiritual discipline and good works. Yet those who seek, seem far more likely to find.

Including those who after a lifetime of breaking their heads on these Christian koans, fall laughing into the arms of God.

What about finding the kin-dom of heaven through a less dramatic form of surrender than a full crash and burn—what if we simply welcomed every experience with trust in the **Grace** of God?

What if we continued to welcome what we would welcome—couldn't that be our key? What if what the saints discovered is that life is a game and we can just play—play our hearts out, enjoying and blessing every moment?

All shall be well, and all shall be well. Every manner of thing will be well.
-- Julian of Norwich, 15th century mystic

As I understand it, Jesus consoled his grief-stricken followers upon his departure by promising something even better to come: universal access in all times and places to the same Spirit that filled his finite human body.

According to the records of Pentecost in the book of Acts, that is just what happened to the first generation of Christians. They found themselves filled with **Joy** and **Love** for all people, fearless of threats to their safety and security, **Inspired** to share the good news, and as fully capable of miracles as their Master.

Even though this spiritual power dedicated to bringing the kin-dom of heaven home to earth seems much attenuated millennia later, it is still present and available. And never limited to those in a particular religious club.

If he came into our temples today, Jesus would probably throw a lot more stuff out.

I say this as a devoted follower of Christ and member of his earthly body, the always-in-need-of-reformation Christian Church.

Those who commit to practicing embodied **Grace** will, however, find ready and useful help in community.

Most people imagine that spiritual community is about sharing blissful experiences with others.

It is actually more like a rock tumbler, where our rough edges are polished smooth in the rough and tumble crucible of life together. The people around you, especially your intimates, will instantly signal (by their own discomfort projected on you) when you may be "out of **Grace**."

Objects in the mirror are closer than they appear

This gives us the awareness and opportunity to self-correct in that moment. That is, if we want to be gracious more than to be right.

Thus do our perceived "enemies" (more accurately, "sanctification coaches") serve our spiritual growth.

The gift of my enemy is that part of me I do not see.
—old Chinese proverb

The power of Corporate Prayer

We can make the fact that humans are highly influenced by those around us work for us. It is well worth seeking out a community of gracious spiritual support because of the contribution you can make and the value you can receive in a field of like-minded aspirants resonating together in the "mind of Christ." My own light may be a bit dim, but a bunch of little LEDs shining together blazes.

Where two or three are gathered in the light or name of Christ, prayers hit home like an arrow that encounters no interference.

"In Christ's Name" is not a magic formula but an invocation of a presence, a vibration. In Jesus' native language, Aramaic, "*name*" can mean light or sound.

Aligning or attuning to Christ's "*name*" can clear away a lot of stumbling blocks and interference between our earthly consciousness and Oneness.

It is important to remember that in the "mind of Christ," we do not insist that "reality" conforms to our limited expectations and perceptions. If I pray only for what I know or want, I won't recognize or allow a better answer.

Prayers "in Christ's Name," while powerful and miraculous in their effects, are launched into the "come what may" or "Thy will be done," of the wider Oneness that Jesus called Father. Which can make for surprising and even more wonderful outcomes!

When our Christ the Healer UCC circle gathers after Sunday Supper there is a moment at the end when people don't seem to want to leave or say anything, as though all the simple movements of the evening—arriving to prepare and share food, conversation, study, prayer and communion—have conjured a sacred space, a holy presence which we can feel, and where we linger to silently revel.

Sometimes we sing:

In this moment, in this place, all is wonder, all is Grace, in this moment, in this place, we are one. —Trisha Watts, "All is Wonder"

Recipes for Abundant Life

The following eight chapters discuss each of the eight states of **Grace** we are naming as points on the **Compass of Grace**: **Acceptance, Gratitude, Joy, Inspiration, Awe, Peace, Presence,** and **Love.**

Reading these chapters is an invitation to re-experience and remember, in your body, when you felt that way before. With practice, you can train your "**Grace** muscle memory" like an athlete to automatically reorient yourself to a state of **Grace** whenever you choose.

You can enter the **Compass of Grace** at any point and read these chapters in any order. We are using these particular words to be able to talk about **Grace,** but the names are somewhat arbitrary and interchangeable.

The value of the words is in their ability to bring a remembered experience palpably present. Thus they function more like invocations than mantras or affirmations. Most of the words invoke manifestations of the "Holy Spirit" as described in the Bible, tapping into those powerful thought forms or morphic fields as well as our personal associations.

If you are more of a visual than a word person, link these words to images that powerfully recall you to the states of **Grace.** If you are more kinesthetic, try expressing postures in your body or hands that evoke the feeling of **Grace.**

In our workshops, we use group exercises including art, music, and movement to help everyone anchor their body feelings so they can be re-accessed at will.

You will likely resonate more strongly with some of these named states than others. This is useful to notice for your further practice, but be assured that upon entering one state, you have access to all of them, for **Grace** is unity.
All of the named states are flavors of Love and Oneness, just as any points we might name on the compasses of "earth" and "hell" are flavors of duality and separation.

Although we encourage memorizing the **Compass of Grace** in the clockwise order given—there is a natural flow from one to the other—each includes all the others and they are inseparable. If any of these words turn the key into the kin-dom of heaven for you, helping you re-orient yourself to a state of **Grace**, they have served their purpose.

For fun as well as your eating pleasure, we have included some of our favorite live food recipes in eight categories along with each **Grace.**

These recipes are the best ones we've developed or adapted since the publication of my first book, The Raw Food Gourmet—Going Raw for Total Well-Being. They've all been tested and featured at Christ the Healer's weekly Sunday Supper gathering, and also include some real winners contributed by our guest chefs. Enjoy!

Chapter 1

Acceptance

Come unto me, all you who labor and who are heavy laden, and I will give you rest. Ask, and it shall be given to you, seek, and you shall find, knock and the door will be opened to you. --Matthew 7:7

There's so much good in the worst of us
And so much bad in the best of us
It doesn't behoove any one of us
To talk about the rest of us
—Edwin Markham

How does it feel to be accepted? *Completely* accepted, unconditionally accepted, by one who knows you and loves you as you are. Bring to mind the person who gave you this gift. Recall a time when you felt accepted.

If you can't remember a time, ask, "If I could remember when I felt this way, what would it be like?" Experience that event in the present moment. Is it a warm feeling, do your shoulders ease, does your breath open? Allow as much detail of the circumstance to be present as though it is happening right now. Mark what you notice for future reference.

My grandmother lived upstairs in a separate apartment in our house during my childhood. Perhaps because I am her namesake, she treated me as a favorite among her grandchildren. Often for hours, I would come in and spread her collection of bells on the couch as she joined me in playing each one. She delighted in my childish delight and never tired of telling me the story of where each bell came from no matter how many times I asked her just to hear her loving voice.

In Grandma's kitchen, I learned the joy of cooking and was encouraged to try any recipe I wanted from her old cookbooks and newspaper clippings. One messy evening we figured out how to make candied grapefruit peel and another time tried our hands at braided candy canes. Even if her door wasn't cracked open, I never doubted my welcome and just barged right in.

Grandma listened thoughtfully whenever I wanted to talk, and never made me feel bad. "Grandma's house" was both a refuge and a magic place of **Acceptance** for me.

Whenever I return to Grandma's house in my imagination, my whole aspect changes. There is a smile on my face, my usually cold hands warm, and any tension drains away.

How does it feel to remember someone's gracious **Acceptance**? Good! It's such a relief.

Maybe you can remember being full of **Acceptance** for someone whose limitations you know quite well, yet hold in your heart this moment without limits—perhaps a child.

Bring that person to mind and let yourself notice what changes in your state of being as you experience yourself being an accepting person. The magic works both ways.

So when have you felt that way before? Can you imagine intensifying that feeling and allowing it to grow? What would it be like to feel accepting or accepted *right now*?

Is there something specific going on in your life that you could practice holding in your heart with **Acceptance**? How could you begin to notice yourself having this feeling of **Acceptance**?

For many, the **Grace** of **Acceptance** may be the easiest point of entry into the **Compass of Grace**.

Acceptance isn't that much of a reach, usually. It simply asks us to be real about what we are experiencing, to notice what we notice without excusing it, and just allow it to be. No stories, no reasons, just **Acceptance** of what we have.

Keep in mind the important difference between approval—a form of judgment— and simple unconditional **Acceptance** of what we perceive to be the facts of the matter, whether we judge them to be good or bad. For some of us may need to practice accepting goodness as well as pain.

Acceptance may begin with reluctant surrender or resignation in the face of unwelcome data, but gracious **Acceptance** grows into an open-hearted "loving what is." Through that, one actually becomes grateful, delighting in "what is" as the **Compass of Grace** takes hold in your life.

Self Awareness

The first step towards growing **Acceptance** of what you habitually reject is to allow yourself to notice current unpleasant feelings and any older suppressed pain you are still carrying in your emotional and physical bodies.

A lifetime habit of reactively pushing away pain may make this difficult.

 Feedback from friends, "enemies," health challenges, and "accidents" gives us the opportunity for greater self-awareness.

Over the years I've learned to develop the enlightening reflex to look into the source of my own reactivity instead of always pushing back whenever someone gets my goat.

 More pro-actively, we can use such things as intuitive decks of cards, games, creative writing,
 sculpting, collage, drawing and painting to peel away layers in order to more honestly face and embrace our hidden selves.

This itself is a form of **Acceptance** that opens the door to more. In our multi-day **Compass of Grace** workshops, we offer experiences of creative "Writing in a State of Grace" and Touch Drawing ™ where feedback from the group encompasses each participant in warm and loving **Acceptance.**

But for some of us, even this first step can be tough. There may be a tendency to hold onto rationalizations, defenses, self understandings, ideas, memories, even people, who reinforce the accommodations we have made to suppressing our painful reality.

I know whereof I speak. Having constructed a perfectionistic personality founded on being seen as a good person—or at least better than those around me—admitting to flaws, let alone sins, seemed to threaten me to the core.

My first big breakthrough towards self awareness came when I studied handwriting analysis and was able to see my fears and defenses literally written on the page in front of me, breaking through my wall of denial.

One workshop participant who struggles with **Acceptance** offers this helpful account:

"I sometimes find that I am not visited by **Acceptance** until after I have steeped in the pain of what is so difficult to accept. So the movement for me is from resistance, to noticing the pain with greater and greater awareness, to **Acceptance.** Sometimes I will just lay in bed, noticing the pain, and softly saying, "Ouch" until the **Grace** of **Acceptance** arrives. That is usually the turning point."

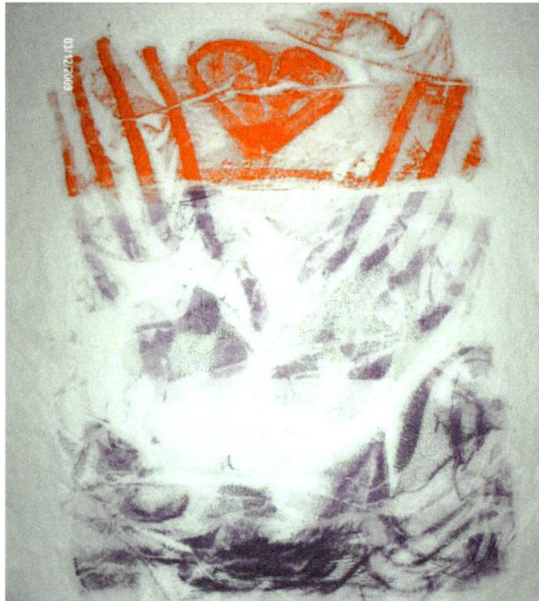

Acceptance
Dana Kelly Sweet

Jesus' powerful parable of the Prodigal Son found in the gospel of Luke is a story of radical **Acceptance**. The father in the story graciously accepts his youngest son's demands to take the money and run, his son's subsequent fall into dissipation, and his ruined, calculating return.

The father also graciously accepts the elder brother's resentment, refusing to qualify his acceptance of either child. We treasure this story for its picture of how Jesus understood the thoroughgoing love of God.

Have you considered that the amount of *"reality"* you can accept amounts to a "rate limit" or ceiling on your quality of life? Can you imagine "raising your roof," accepting more, being more alive?

Self Love

As you welcome the grace of **Acceptance** into your life, remember to include *self-acceptance*. For myself and many I know, it is easier to accept almost anyone else besides myself. Of course, *I* know my sorry record better than anyone but God, and am holding a more profound list of judgments and unforgivable sins against myself than anyone else possibly could.

Why is this? It appears to be an ancient twist in our psychologies. Layers of scar tissue covering the infant's wound and unspoken cry: "Do I belong here? Am I worthy of love?" If I judge myself harder than anyone else, I feel some control over that terrifying vulnerability, doing unto myself before anyone can do unto me what I believe I must deserve.

For those of us who have given up on trying to "be good," holding on to self-hate and self-loathing feels like the punishment we secretly believe we deserve.

The difficulty of loving oneself may be compounded by familial, cultural, and/or religious training that inculcates self condemnation, self-blame and guilt to control selfish behavior.

But does it ever work to curse the darkness? Does adding hate to what is already hateful change its state? Does the God of Jesus hate sinners or teach us to forgive?

And if I am willing to forgive others but not myself, isn't that just a face of pride, imagining that I am different, special, and worse than everyone else?

Forgiveness

Forgiveness is not approval, but a form of active **Acceptance** through release and surrender of a "still playing" loop of resistance and resentment about the original grievance.

We have a saying at Christ the Healer that "Forgiveness is remedial love."
If I failed to love and embrace that first moment of pain in any circumstance, if I resisted in the form of anger, fear, grief, apathy, or unconsciousness, then I took damage to my human operating system.

And now I am most likely reinforcing it with some self-righteous story about what happened, creating enemies in my mind and threatening to go deeper and deeper into **Self Protection**. Becoming less and less alive, healthy, sane. More in a bind.

Admit it, this doesn't feel good.

In our Body Electronics practice, when we hit a wall of resistance to forgiveness or self forgiveness that seems insurmountable, we often break through it by asking, "Can you forgive...Are you willing to forgive...if not, are you *willing to be willing* to forgive?"

Love heals, and forgiveness applies the balm of love to existing damage.

Ideally we might rise to such a level of day to day **Acceptance** in meeting each circumstance that no new damage occurs and nothing need be forgiven.

Instead of having to forgive after you've judged something unacceptable and gone into **Self Protection** around it, can you imagine *giving for(ward)* to each new day the permission that it be acceptable to you? And then you could "forgive" or give forward to yourself the permission to graciously **Accept** whatever comes as a gift.

> *"Let he who is without sin cast the first stone...Is there no one to condemn you? Neither do I condemn you. Go, and sin no more."* --John 8:11

****

Green Smoothies

I imagine green smoothies, a synergistic combination of blended fruit, water and greens, to be the modern food that embodies **Acceptance.**

First, nearly everyone likes and can digest fruit. Second, green smoothies are forgiving as the easily assimilable nutrients and fiber broken down by the blender can heal damaged digestive systems.

Further, research has shown that of all foods, dark leafy greens such as kale contain the closest match in number and proportion to the known nutritional needs of our bodies, including protein.

We have also seen that our nearest genetic relations, the chimps, thrive on a diet consisting mostly of seasonal greens and fruit.

So why not blend the two in satisfying combinations to nurture our physical health?

Blending fresh greens and fruit releases those powerful phytochemicals more effectively than cooking, making them easily bio-available while still keeping the foods whole and the nutrients undamaged.

We all have Victoria Boutenko to thank for this 21st century update on optimal nourishment for our animal bodies.

She is the one who discovered that greens were the missing virtue in nearly all diets, including raw food ones. Her research has demonstrated that the healing and detoxification effects of simply adding a daily green smoothie to whatever else you might be eating will show up in a month or less.

Since being introduced to them from Victoria, Thomas and I have demonstrated a profound level of **Acceptance** for our physical bodies' needs by treating green smoothies as our "daily bread."

It's easy, fun--and if you use enough fruit—always tastes good. Given the variety and abundance of fruits and greens, you could amuse yourself endlessly discovering tasty combinations.

Inspired by Victoria, I have made a special study of lesser known wild and cultivated greens and weeds to add further variety and nutrition. (See my list below.)

For best results, consider acquiring a high speed blender such as a VitaMix or Blend-Tec, as they have the power to pulverize the toughest leaves and fruits into a satisfying smoothie in just seconds. Lower powered blenders will also work, but you will have to chop things more finely before you blend.

The basic procedure is this: Put filtered water in your blender first—more or less depending on how thick you like your smoothie. Then add your chopped up fruit and greens in any proportion.

Start with lots more fruit than greens, at least a 2 to 1 ratio by volume, and adjust to your taste.

Experiment with substituting different fruits or combinations you like. Organic fruit in season, especially locally grown is the best choice. To keep your smoothie smooth, you can include a fruit with soluble fiber like mango, blueberries, cranberries, peach, pineapple, nectarine, pear, persimmon, durian, or avocado instead of relying only on bananas. Without that your smoothie will only be smooth if you drink it right away or stir it up after it sits.

It's vital to your success that you like the taste of green smoothies enough so that they become the foundation of your daily food intake.

We found that by starting slowly, just a small handful of spinach or a stick of celery or a couple pieces of lettuce in a blender full of water and fruit, we quickly began craving more greens and the proportions changed.

Now we initiate our friends with Beginner Smoothies while imbibing more daring concoctions at home. Experiment with all the organic greens you can find, including kale, chard, cilantro, basil, mint, collards, bok choy, celery, parsley, romaine, and red and green lettuces. Buy or grow sprouts such as alfalfa, pea, and sunflower, especially in the winter when greens at the store aren't so fresh. Vary your greens and fruits seasonally like the chimps for full spectrum nutrition and also so you don't get sick of one combination.

I learned this the hard way by drinking only banana-kale smoothies my first 3 months until I couldn't look at another leaf of kale without feeling revolted.

This is actually a healthy reaction to over-accumulation of the low-level phytotoxins in all greens put there by the plant in a co-creative effort to ensure diversity in the herbivore diet.

Here's a couple of our best recipes to get your own (green) juices flowing:

Beginner Smoothie
Thomas and I call this a "beginner smoothie" because it was the first one we tried at Victoria Boutenko's suggestion. Simplicity itself, the uninitiated find it surprisingly enjoyable despite the unusual green color.

2 c filtered water
2 ripe bananas, peeled and chopped
1 large handful organic spinach

Blend water and fruit. Add spinach and blend until smooth.

Berry Smoothie

In midsummer Oregon, we are blessed to find local strawberries, raspberries, blackberries and blueberries all ripe at the same time. Ah, the anti-oxidants!

2 c filtered water
4 c mixed fresh berries, including some blueberries
1 small head red lettuce

Blend water and fruit first. Add greens and blend until smooth.

Pear Grape Smoothie

A fall favorite. This one is sweet enough to override the bitterness of dandelion.

1 bunch grapes, washed and de-stemmed
1 ripe pear
Handful of dandelion greens, washed
Filtered water to blend

Variation: replace the grapes with another pear and 1 c organic cranberries

Blend water and fruit. Add green and blend until smooth

Green Stinger Smoothie

Wild stinging nettles (Urtica species) begin poking through the ground of rich woods in February here in Oregon. They are available summer until frost watered and pinched back in my own garden, furnishing one of the most valuable greens known for your green smoothies.

Fear not, the stinging hairs are completely neutralized by blending, and until that stage you can use gloves for harvesting and rinsing.

Stinging nettles provided a lesson in self-mastery when I fell into a patch of them chasing my dog.

Not much before that, I had endured a long and difficult labor and delivery without drugs by learning self-hypnosis. It occurred to me in that moment of fear and agony in the nettles that I could replay myself hypnosis tape in my head. As I did so, I began to relax and then watched in amazement as the blisters on my reddened hand re-sorbed within a few minutes.

*In our Body Electronics practice, we learn that the difference between nerve signal and pain is something we create through our resistance to or loving **Acceptance** of bodily stimulation.*

*Now I joyfully pick stinging nettles barehanded and there is no pain or blistering—just an enlivening tingle. When you have learned their secret (welcoming nettles in a state of **Grace**), you can pluck a leaf when you come upon them, roll it up, pop it in your mouth, and enjoy its fresh green gift even without a blender!*

1 large handful of stinging nettle tops, rinsed (remove the toughest stems)
2 oranges, peeled and chopped
1 c plum, grapes, pear, or apple in bite sized pieces

Add filtered water to blend to desired consistency.

Wild Green Smoothie

Foraging is fun, especially if all you have to do is step outside and see what's growing around you. I encourage certain garden volunteers: dandelion, plantain, chickweed, malva, lambs quarters, amaranth, and purslane among them.

Here's a list of over 100 garden greens, herbs, weeds, and natives that have gone into my blender—some as a matter of desperation when nothing else was growing. Be smart and start one at a time with small quantities to see if your taste buds or your body have a negative reaction. Make sure you have the right plant as common names vary. Consult books and experts to be certain. And please email me if you find something good that's not on this list.

Get to know the edible and poisonous plants in your area before you experiment!

---

alfalfa sprouts, aloe leaf, amaranth, artichoke leaf, Asian greens, asparagus
bedstraw (cleavers), bamboo leaves, beet greens, bergamot (monarda), blueberry leaves, bok choy, borage leaves and flowers, buckwheat "lettuce"
cactus, calendula flowers and leaves, cardoon leaves, carrot tops, cats ear, celery, chard, chenopodiums, chervil, chickweed (stellaria), cilantro, clover, collard, comfrey flowers and leaves, cucumber leaves
dandelion
endive, evening primrose leaves and flowers
fennel, fig leaves, filaree, fireweed

gingko leaves, good king henry, goji (wolfberry) leaves, grape leaves

hibiscus leaves, horsetail, hosta

Japanese maple young leaves, Jerusalem artichoke new growth

kale, knotweed, lamium weed

lambs quarters, lapsana communis (nipplewort), lavatera flowers and leaves, lemon balm, lettuces, linden tree leaves, lovage

mache, mallow (malva), marshmallow, miner's lettuce, mint, mizuna, mouse ear chickweed (cerastium), mulberry leaves

Napa cabbage, nettle

oca leaves, orach, oxalis, oxeye daisy flowers and leaves

parsley, young pine and spruce needles, plantain, pumpkin or squash leaves, purslane

quinoa leaves

red clover flowers, rose leaves

salad burnet, scorzonera leaves, seaweed, sheep sorrel, shiso, snap peas, garden sorrel, stevia, strawberry leaves and tops, sunflower sprouts, sweet cicely, sweet potato sprouts, salsify

turnip greens

valerian leaves, violet leaves and flowers

watercress, watermelon leaves, wheat grass

yacon leaf, yellow dock

Good enough to eat!

Chapter 2

Gratitude

Give thanks in all circumstances.
--1 Thessalonians 5:18

For all that has been, thanks. For all that will be, yes.
--Dag Hammarskjold

Gratitude—a foundational and accessible grace, perhaps even a familiar feeling—comes from the same root as the word that gives us grace—*gratis.*

Gratitude, like all the graces, is free and unconditional. It is a state of being, not dependent upon outer conditions. To only be grateful for what we like or want is at best limited appreciation, and at worst, dismissive and judgmental towards what and whom we don't prefer.

Yet counting our blessings and being thankful for good things is a useful beginning step towards unconditional **Gratitude.** As we exercise our imaginations in expanding the list of what we're grateful for, a tipping point comes when we fall into a state of simply feeling **Gratitude,** being **Gratitude.**

Then we can bring that state of mind into heart, flesh and muscle and notice how it feels be truly grateful for future reference.

For instance, we give thanks for our food, and sometimes also remember to be grateful for those involved in the food's journey to our table, the growers and distributors.

What if we also gave thanks *to* the food, honoring it for giving its life for us?

All life nourishes other life. Even we humans, at the top of the food chain, feed insects and bacteria in our living bodies, and when we are done with our flesh coats, they become grist for the alchemists milling the soil.

Being grateful to your food acknowledges the relationship and allows us to appreciate more of its qualities, deepening the communion.

For the farmer
For the land
For the kitchen's practiced hand
For the food's life gift of love
God within, with us, above
We give thanks —CtH Notebook of Words

This wisdom is found in the Buddhist focus on mindful eating as well as in the Christian sacrament of Holy Communion. *Eucharist,* the ancient word for the sacrament, means "thanksgiving" in Greek. Jesus instituted the sacrament of communion as a daily physical reminder of **Grace,** giving, and oneness.

The great challenge to embodied as opposed to theoretical oneness, of course, is the difficulty of getting along in real life and relationships.

"Hell is other people" as the saying goes. Which is why Jesus invited us to love our enemies and bless those who curse us.

If you aspire to the fullness of **Grace,** there is an advanced **Gratitude** practice that can get you there. I was first introduced to the idea in a book called *Thank You For Being Such a Pain* by Mark Rosen. Another good resource is the "Work" of Byron Katie. In Body Electronics we call it "Verbal Point Holding."

My personal method is to begin with a prayer asking for help, because this level of work goes against all cultural programming and seemingly natural reactions.

Next, review your current relationships and find one where you are the victim as you see it. Do you find yourself obsessing or complaining about a certain person over and over?

Notice how strongly justified you feel in judging them for what they did or didn't do or are doing to you. Can you let go of your attachment to the story?

Ask yourself, "What hurts?" What is the pain hiding under my angry resistance to this person?

Perhaps it is deeply buried and actually has more to do with an older memory that the recent offense just triggered, or a long series of similar hurts.

Ask yourself, "Do I want to heal this pain that has now come to light thanks to the person I am dancing the dance of **Self Protection** with?

Can I be grateful to the one whose painful sacrifice has brought my own crusted-over wounds to light where they can be seen, loved and healed?

Can I allow this felt **Gratitude** to shift me from the state of hell to **Grace, Peace, Acceptance**?"

I'm not saying it's easy or comfortable, but it does work. It is beautiful to be around someone who truly embodies loving their enemies.

I have no enemies, for I make them my friends.--Abraham Lincoln

"Body of Christ"
Dana Kelley Sweet

One bread, one body
One source of all
One cup of blessing that we share
And we, though many, throughout the world
We are one body in this one bread
--John Foley, S.J., adapted

Moving from ordinary "**Getting Along**" states of consciousness to **Gratitude** is a *metanoia,* a shift in consciousness, that you can easily track and practice. So remember, imagine, when have you been grateful?

How does it feel in your body to be grateful? Relief, burdens slipping off your shoulders?

What was the circumstance that allowed you to notice how grateful you felt? Bring your memories of deep, abiding **Gratitude** forward and play them in your mind's eye.

For many, **Gratitude** will be one of the octants on the **Compass of Grace** that is easiest to access. That is because children are encouraged to be grateful, whereas they may be discouraged from exuberant expressions of **Joy** and **Awe.**

Perhaps you, as I, learned **Gratitude** best upon being rescued from a situation where you felt powerless and a sense of impending doom.

On what should have been my joyous graduation day from Yale college, I was depressed because my boyfriend had dumped me some weeks earlier after taking up with someone else. In an emotional downspin, I had stopped attending one of my classes and then skipped the final exam, leaving me short one semester hour of credits to get the degree I had worked on for four years.

Frankly, I didn't give a damn. After listlessly wandering the festive campus and feeling very sorry for myself, I returned to my room to find a message from the dean of my residential college.

Unknown to me, he had noticed my lapse, called a music professor whose yearlong course I had dropped after getting a "D" the first semester, and persuaded her to give me one hour of credit for my poor work, bending the rules to allow me to graduate.

A "gift 'D'," he called it. I have this kind man to thank for the Yale sheepskin on my wall and resume.

Remembering how we were on the receiving end of **Grace** is one door through which to enter the **Compass of Grace.** It's not hard for me to retrieve other memories of when I was given another chance, no thanks to anything I did to deserve it.

Remember Scrooge when he woke from his nightmare with the Ghost of Christmas Future to find he wasn't dead yet? Yes! A reprieve, a new beginning after a loss or threatened loss, grateful just to be alive.

****

Gratitude can be very sweet. Which is why the recipes in this chapter feature healthy raw desserts. For more dessert recipes, check the chapters on **Awe** ("superfood" desserts) and **Presence** (dehydrator treats)

Sweet Appetizers and Dessert

The simplest desserts can be the best. Here are some presentation ideas for fresh fruit in season:

Mandala of apple slices sprinkled with cinnamon and/or grated ginger
    Cantaloupe slices with grated nutmeg
    Watermelon slices with lime wedges
    Fresh strawberries with chopped tarragon
    Sliced cantaloupe-strawberry "sandwiches" sprinkled with lime
    Strawberries filling a cantaloupe-half basket
    Fresh sliced figs with grated cardamom on a plate lined with fig leaves
    Orange half-slice "smiles" with fennel seeds and chopped mint
    Frozen grapes, melon and banana chunks

Jeweled Fruit Parfait—in a pretty glass with orange chunks, banana, kiwi and pomegranate seeds

Fruit Kabobs—pineapple, mango, kiwi, grape, strawberry, banana, avocado, tangerine on a stick (Can also freeze after assembling and serve cold)

Rainbow Snow-- blended fresh blueberry, blackberry, strawberry, raspberry, kiwi, mango syrup on shaved ice

Medjool dates—pitted and stuffed with pecan halves or raw almond butter

Seedlings

Easy and fun to make with kids.

4 medjool dates, pitted
¼ c raisins
3 T each unhulled sesame, hulled sunflower, and hulled pumpkin seed

Mix with S blade in food processor. Form into a 1" diameter log and slice into 8 pieces.

Apricot Fruit Sauce

Our friend Samantha created this rich tasting sauce for a Moroccan-themed Sunday Supper. She drizzled it over orange slices for an amazing, satisfying dessert. You could also use it for a dipping sauce.

1 c dried apricots, chopped, soaked in 2 c water for an hour or so
juice of 1 lemon
2 t cinnamon
½ t each ground nutmeg, allspice, cardamom and ginger
pomegranate seeds and chopped mint, optional, for garnish

Blend everything together. Add filtered water as needed. Spoon over fresh orange slices just before serving.

Smooth Move Pudding

Thomas invented (and named) this when we were looking for a simple, digestible dessert to accompany a fairly heavy raw gourmet menu. A garnish improves the appearance, but there's nothing unappetizing about the bright, refreshing taste.

10 juicy oranges
1 lb dried pitted prunes
filtered water
mint leaves or pomegranate seeds, optional, to garnish

Squeeze half of the oranges and put the juice with prunes to soak for 2-24 hours in the refrigerator. When ready, combine with the rest of the peeled oranges. Blend, adding water as needed for a pudding consistency. Pour into pretty serving cups and top with garnish.

Chiaoca Pudding

Chia seeds swell up somewhat like tapioca to thicken this pudding. It tastes good with fresh berries. You can add ¼ c raw cacao powder for chocolate chia pudding.

2 c soaked raw almonds for milk
4 c filtered water
1 c raw cashews, soaked for 1 hour
1/4 c agave syrup or coconut nectar or equivalent in pitted dates--about 1/2 c
1 vanilla bean
1/2 c chia seeds
1/4 c extra virgin coconut oil
 sprinkle of unprocessed salt, optional

Drain the almonds and blend with fresh water to make 4 c of almond milk. You can leave in the pulp or strain it out. Blend in cashews, sweetener, and vanilla bean. Add chia and mix well. Wait 15 minutes or more until the chia seed have expanded, then blend in the rest of the ingredients.

Apple Crisp

10 organic apples, seeded and chopped (leave peel on)
2 cups walnuts (preferably soaked several hours, rinsed, and re-dried)
8 pitted medjool dates
1 t cinnamon

Pulse dates and walnuts together in a food processor until mixed but not blended. Set aside in another bowl. Blend 4 of the apples in the food processor with cinnamon to make a sauce. Set aside. Using the slicer blade of the processor or a knife, thinly slice the remaining apples and place in 9x12 baking pan. Pour on the sauce and hand mix. Crumble date-nut mixture on top and press in lightly. Warm in a dehydrator for a few hours or serve immediately.

Carrot Cake Bars

This makes enough for 8-12 people to have seconds. They will want to.

<u>Crust</u>
3 c walnuts, soaked overnight, rinsed, and dehydrated until dry
1 c dates, pitted

Process walnut pieces in a food processor with the S blade until fairly fine. Pulse in dates until blended. Mixture should be clumping together. If not, add a few drops of water. Press mixture into 9x12' pan.

<u>Filling</u>
2 lbs. carrots washed and chopped
1 ½ c raisins
1 T fresh ginger, grated
1 t cardamom, ground
1 t cinnamon, ground
½ t nutmeg

Process carrots in a food processor with the S blade until finely grated. Pulse in spices until thoroughly mixed. Pulse in raisins until roughly chopped. Spread over crust in pan.

<u>Icing</u>
1 c cashews, soaked for an hour and drained
juice of one orange
1 t vanilla water or extract
2 dates or other raw sweetener

Blend together in a blender. Mixture should be as thick as possible. Add more orange juice if needed to blend. Spread over filling and refrigerate until ready to serve.

Caramel Apple Dip

Rich party dip that you can make fast and be proud to take anywhere.

1 cup pine nuts
½ cup pitted soft dates
¼ c extra virgin coconut oil

Blend everything together in a food processor until smooth. Add filtered water as needed.

Caramel Apple Dip

Chapter 3

Joy

But the angel said, "Do not be afraid. I bring you good news of great joy for all the people."
--Luke 2:10

Gratitude can overflow into delighted **Joy. Joy** can also surprise us in an ordinary or even painful moment.

For true **Joy**, like **Love,** is unconditional. Pleasure and happiness depend on circumstances. **Joy** is always present whether recognized or not, for **Joy** needs no reason.

Joy sparkles like a diamond that is unaffected by its surroundings, although it can seem most wondrous when set in pain.

> *I saw raindrops on my window*
> *joy is like the rain*
> *laughter runs across my pane*
> *slips away and comes again*
> *joy is like the rain*
> *--Miriam Therese Winter*

Many, many a funeral or memorial service where I have officiated has erupted in tears of **Joy** and laughter at some point as the participants recalled stories about their loved one, often with the dead body sitting right in front of them.

> *Joy is the surest sign of the presence of God*
> --Pierre Teilhard de Chardin

Joy can be welcomed. When welcomed and received, it can also grow.

Interestingly, **Joy** is the higher octave of desire, of wanting and struggle to have, found in the **Compass of Getting Along**.

Many of us fill our hours (and living spaces) with getting things that we think we want, and pushing away what we don't want, but somehow we never seem to get what we *really* want, which is to be loved for ourselves.

We create relationships based on what our wounds tell us we need and want. Always a negotiation with what the others need and want, these relationships never satisfy us fully.

Imagine instead that your path to **Love** that is unconditional, not the love of connection, desire, approval—is through **Joy**.

What if you welcomed whatever may come that you do not want by taking **Joy** in it instead of contracting in resistance? **Joy** in being alive, in being able to feel something, anything, in your body even if it is a heartache or physical pain.

Take **Joy.** Be inspired. What happens if you are joyous enough to be inspired? If you are inspired, you behave differently.

That will help proceed you around the **Compass of Grace**, and you may even discover a way to accept what is unwanted in yourself and others with unconditional **Love.**

I have a dear friend who often experiences her life as stressful and overwhelming. She taught me a way to find **Joy** and avoid going into **Self Protection** when life feels threatening.

She looks for and then focuses on something in the mess that she can smile about. Her brave choice to smile ignites smiles on other faces, which beam back, surrounding her with **Joy** that she can then take in.

Here is a **Joy**-spreading song she shared, sung to the tune of Auld Lang Syne. Sing along with me as you read it and see if your human operating system lightens up a bit:

A smile is quite a funny thing,
It wrinkles up your face,
And when it's gone you'll never find
Its secret hiding place.

But far more wonderful it is
To see what smiles can do,
You smile at one, he smiles at you,
And so one smile makes two.

To access your body memories of **Joy**, allow yourself to notice how you're feeling in your body right now. How your bones and muscles feel, your skin, eyes, mouth, feet, hands, scalp, breathing, and whatever else you can be aware of as physical sensation. Relax, and invite joyful memories to arise. Pick one when you felt **Joy** before and bring in as much detail as possible as though you were there now.

How old are you? Is it night or day? Are you alone or are others present? What are you wearing? What is happening? What is your emotional tone? How is your body responding, your posture, your breath, facial expression, the tension or release in your muscles? Notice, just notice what you notice.

Now allow yourself to intensify the body-emotional memory of **Joy**. Bring it right into your bind. Allow it to grow.

I think of my youngest son, who was born with a rare auto immune disease that showed up as I weaned him to baby food and formula, neither of which he could tolerate. Eventually we figured out he could thrive on a wheat, dairy, sugar and artificial chemical-free diet supplemented with immune supporting herbs. Instead of the wasting away waif he had been, Gil grew into a golden little Adonis whose beauty, life force, and charisma put fellow school children in the shade. Just remembering Gil's *joie de vivre*—whether racing his tricycle, diving, dancing, or juggling a soccer ball—brings back a warm feeling and all over smile to my heart.

How does **Joy** feel to you? Note if there is one place in your body where it seems to be focused. Let the **Joy** spread to the rest of you from there.

When we do this exercise in a room full of people, we watch the group for who lights up and invite them to share their memory. Quite often, someone describes being present at a childbirth. Inevitably, this triggers smiles and memories in the rest of us until the room itself feels charged with **Joy.**

Heartburst
Dana Kelly Sweet

The morning stars sang together and all the angels shouted for joy—Job 38:7

****

Our recipes for **Joy** include lovely salads, artfully arranged gifts of nature that sings with **Joy** all around us. Enjoy!

Edible flower mandala

Collect edible flowers in season and arrange on a round plate for an edible centerpiece or a fragrant first course. Here's a surprisingly long list of edible flowers to expand your horizons.

alkanet, (anchusa), anise hyssop, apple blossoms, arugula
basil, bee balm, black locust blossoms, borage
calendula, California poppy, carnation, chamomile, chives, chrysanthemum, citrus, coriander, clover (white and red), cornflower
dame's rocket, dandelion, dahlia, day lily, dill, daisy
elderberry, empress tree, (Paulownia) evening primrose
fennel, forsythia, fuchsia
gardenia, garlic, gladiolus
hollyhock, hosta, hibiscus, honeysuckle
impatiens
jasmine, Johnny jump up
lavatera, lavender, leek, lemon verbena, lilac
magnolia, mallow, marigold, meadow sweet, mint, mustard family
nasturtium
okra
pansy, peony, pineapple guava, primrose
Queen Ann's lace
redbud, rose, rosemary
safflower, sage, salsify, scarlet runner bean, scented geranium, self heal, snapdragon, society garlic, squash, strawberry, sunflower
tuberous begonia, tulip
violet
yucca

Be sure they are organically grown and free of bugs. Some lend themselves to sweet dishes, others to savory. Some look better than they taste. Be certain of your identification before eating, and start with a little nibble.

Avoid known poisonous blooms such as autumn crocus, buttercup, clematis, daffodil, delphinium, foxglove, hyacinth, hydrangea, iris, larkspur, lily of the valley, mandevilla, monkshood, morning glory, oleander, poinsettia, rhododendron, Star of Bethlehem, sweet pea, wisteria.

Mesclun Salad with Edible Flowers

I actually plant parrot tulips each year just so I can serve them in a spring salad with magnolias, which bloom about the same time. The petals look spectacular and taste a lot like lettuce. Commonly available summer flowers like nasturtium, pansies, and calendula petals can light up this salad, too.

Combine a bag of mesclun greens or your own mix in a large salad bowl. Toss with lemon juice, extra virgin olive oil, a little balsamic vinegar (optional and not raw) and unprocessed salt to taste. Just before serving, gently toss in several handfuls of edible flowers, leaving a few on top for decoration.

Greek Salad

Just to remind you that a good Greek salad is already raw.

2 heads romaine, chopped
½ red onion sliced thin
1 cucumber sliced
2-4 ripe tomatoes chopped
10-12 sun dried or naturally brined olives
¼ c lemon juice
¼ c extra virgin olive oil
1 T chopped fresh or 1 t dried oregano
unprocessed salt and fresh ground pepper to taste

1 clove of garlic, optional, to rub in the salad bowl before tossing the greens with the dressing

Place all ingredients in a large serving bowl. Add dressing ingredients and toss.

Fresh Herb Ranch with Red Lettuce

This rich and universally popular dressing also makes a great veggie dip.

2 heads red lettuce, washed and torn into bite sized pieces
1 c soaked cashews
1 c soaked sunflower seeds
6 stalks celery chopped
1 cucumber, chopped (remove peel if bitter)
½ c lemon juice
¼ c extra virgin olive oil
¼ c fresh dill chopped
couple sprigs fresh basil
½ t onion powder
½ t garlic powder
½-1 t unprocessed salt
2 dates, pitted
1 T raw apple cider vinegar
filtered water to blend
black pepper to taste

Put leaves in serving bowl. Combine olive oil, lemon juice and vinegar with celery and cucumber in blender and liquefy. Add the rest of the ingredients and blend to desired consistency. Serve on the side with lettuce salad or chopped vegetables for dipping.

Jennifer Salad

Adapted from a dish a friend brought to a raw potluck. Simple, fast, impressive, and no oil needed.

2 bunches spinach, stems removed
½ t unprocessed salt
2 T lemon juice
½ c raisins
½ c pine nuts
optional festive garnish: pomegranate seeds.

Soak raisins in lemon juice for at least ½ hr. Rinse and spin spinach leaves and place in bowl. Sprinkle salt over leaves and gently massage to begin releasing juices. Stir in raisin mixture and top and strew pine nuts all over. Serve right away.

Mac-Cheeze Salad

We've been enjoying this every summer when the zucchinis burgeon ever since our friend Shanti Moon of Nourishing Elements introduced it at the 2010 Raw and Living Spirit Retreat. If you have a vegetable spiralizer for the zucchini, it becomes a noodle salad. Makes a large bowl, but leftovers are unlikely if you take it to a potluck.

5 medium zucchini, spiralized or cut in small bite sized chunks
1 bunch celery, chopped small
2 sweet or red onions, diced
2 pints cherry tomatoes, cut in half
1 bunch tat soy or other dark leafy green such as spinach, washed and chopped
3 red, orange or yellow bell peppers, diced

Variations: fresh corn cut off the cob, broccoli or cauliflower, cut into small pieces

Dressing
1 c raw macadamia nuts
juice of 1 lemon
1 inch section fresh ginger, grated
1 inch piece of fresh turmeric or 1 T dried powder
5 pitted dates
1 T curry powder
½ -1 t cayenne to taste
unprocessed salt, to taste

Filtered water to blend

Prepared the vegetables and combine in a large serving bowl. Blend dressing ingredients and mix with vegetables.

Fresh Tahini Dressing

*Use this bright lemony sauce over **Falafel** or just tomatoes and greens. You can make this ahead of time as it holds its flavor in the fridge for up to a week.*

½ c unhulled sesame seeds, soaked 2-8 hours (will expand to about 1 c)
1 ½ c filtered water
¼ c fresh lemon juice
1 t unprocessed salt

Rinse soaked seeds and blend with other ingredients until smooth.

Holy Kale Salad

Perfected from a popular salad making the rounds of our local food coop by our friend Brion Oliver who packaged it for the raw gourmet trade at our farmers market. Keeps well in the fridge for a few days. Exceptionally good as a filling for an onion bread fold over sandwich! (see page 96 for onion bread recipe)

3 large bunches kale, washed stemmed and chopped
1 c raw sesame tahini
¼ c Nama Shoyu or Coconut Aminos
2 T raw apple cider vinegar
1 inch piece ginger peeled and minced
2-3 cloves garlic minced

Massage everything together in a large bowl. Best after an hour or more for the kale to soften.

Variation: If you process everything in a food processor, you'll have a stunning kale pesto instead.

Grain free Tabouli

Satisfies my memories of Lebanese home cooking without the cooking or couscous. If your garden or Mexican market gives you purslane (verdolargo) in the summer, you can include it and increase your omega 3 fatty acid intake quite deliciously.

2 cucumbers, diced
2 ripe tomatoes, chopped
1 bunch parsley, chopped
1 bunch mint, chopped
1/3 c lemon juice
1/3 c extra virgin olive oil
unprocessed salt to taste

optional: purslane, chopped

Toss everything together and enjoy.

Waldorf Salad Sans Mayo

A simpler oil-free version of the Waldorf Salad with Almond Mayonnaise in my first book.

4 organic apples seeded and diced with peel
¼ c lemon juice
1 bunch celery, diced
1 lb. grapes—cut in half if large
1 c chopped walnuts

optional: seeds from 1 pomegranate

Toss everything together in a bowl and serve.

Salsa Salad

A creamy hybrid of guacamole and salsa that has everyone coming back for seconds.

1 bunch cilantro, chopped
½ onion, diced
½ jalapeno, minced, 1 clove garlic, minced
2 green onions, chopped
1 cucumber chopped
2 tomatoes, chopped
¼ c lemon or lime juice
2 ripe avocados, peeled, seeded, chopped
½- 1 t unprocessed salt

Mash the avocados with a fork, and stir into the rest . Serve immediately.

Fennel Slice Salad

Salads don't have to be leaves. This colorful combination of vegetables is crunchy and satisfying.

1 bulb fennel, sliced
1 cucumber, chopped
1 red pepper sliced
1 carrot, chopped
½ bulb of celeriac thinly sliced, or 2 sticks celery chopped
2 T apple cider vinegar
2 T extra virgin olive oil
unprocessed salt and ground black pepper to taste

Mix together in a serving bowl. Toss with oil and vinegar, salt and pepper.

Kale Chiffonade with Almond Herb Dressing

Chiffonade, French for "cut into rags," is a knife technique that makes tough Brassicas like kale, collards, and Brussels sprouts much more edible raw.

2 bunches of kale, de-stemmed

Wash kale and roll enough leaves together to make a tight bundle. Starting at the end farthest from your hand holding the bundle together, shear across and down through the roll repeatedly until all the kale is reduced to thin ribbons. Massage in 1 cup Almond Herb dressing, recipe below. Kale will be a bit more tender if allowed to marinate an hour before serving

Brazil Nut Rawmesan

½ c Brazil nuts
1 clove garlic
1 t unprocessed salt

Whiz this all up in a food processor for a few seconds until just crumbly but not blended. Store in a jar in the fridge for up to several weeks.

Salad toppings

*Increase the interest and nutrition of your salads by adding some of these: edible flowers, chopped herbs, sprouted sunflower seeds, sesame seeds, sprouted lentils, onion bread crumbs, pomegranate seeds, dehydrated spiced seeds and nuts. You can also quickly make some **Brazil Nut Rawmesan**, above, to sprinkle on top.*

Almond Herb dressing
This is equally good mixed into shredded red and green cabbage for a coleslaw.

1 c dry raw almonds, soaked 4-8 hours, rinsed, and drained (can substitute soaked hulled sunflower seeds for half of the almonds)
¼ c raw apple cider vinegar
juice of one lemon
½-1 c filtered water
¼ c extra virgin olive oil
1 T salt free Italian herb blend with garlic
½-1 t unprocessed salt
ground black pepper to taste

Put everything in a blender, beginning with half of the water and blend. Add more water as needed and adjust seasonings.

Napa Slaw

1 head Napa (Asian) cabbage, washed and sliced into thin strips
2 apples, cored and diced
1 cup celery, diced
2 green onions chopped fine
1 small red onion, diced

Dressing
1T raw apple cider vinegar
juice of 2 lemons
1 c cashews, soaked for an hour and drained
unprocessed salt and black pepper to taste.

Blend until creamy. Toss with prepared veggies, above.

Food Art

For a number of years CtH UCC offered this popular activity at a children's peace fair, where so many of the other booths featured sugary treats. We handed each child a paper plate for their canvas, washed their hands, and set them down at a table containing bowls of sprouts, cherry tomatoes, jicama, sliced red cabbage, red and yellow pepper, snap peas, cucumbers, mint, basil, parsley, cilantro, mini carrots, and other eye-appealing vegetables. Like little Tibetan monks, they created their mandalas of the moment, admired them, and then they were gone.

Play With Your Food

Chapter 4

Inspiration

The Lord God formed the human from the dust of the earth and breathed into his nostrils the breath of life and the man became a living being—Genesis 2:7

Joy bursts the fetters of the small self allowing us to breathe fully.

Inspiration literally means to breathe.

Here's an exercise that opens your chest and aligns your spine: Relax your shoulders, look up, stretch your arms and hands to the point your eyes have chosen; breathe.

Keeping your eyes up, lower your arms to your sides and repeat the breathe-reach twice more. On the last lowering of arms, you finally, without moving your head, focus your eyes forward.

Now adjust your head forward, feeling your back align and your chest expand. Try breathing again and see if you notice a change. If you do this exercise standing, as we demonstrate in our workshops, you will experience your body as though it were hanging from a plumb line, which is how it is designed to be held.

Breathing oxygenates and energizes our bodies, increasing our liveliness.

Conversely, we limit our ability to breathe fully when our bodies contract in emotional resistance and self-defense.

> *Breathe on me, breath of God*
> *Fill me with life anew*
> *That I may love the way you love*
> *And do what you would do*
> *—Edwin Hatch*

In Christian tradition, the Holy Spirit is compared to the wind as well as the breath of God. In Eastern traditions, this presence is known as *prana, chi,* or *ki.* Pervading all, the Spirit represents God immanent, or within everything, the third person of the Trinity.

The creating, renewing energy of spirit is most obvious in the power of nature when we allow ourselves to notice. When human nature is inspired, we recognize that as creativity or being in the flow.

One thing that may stop us from being in the flow of inspiration is performance anxiety. Artists and athletes alike report they perform best when they forget themselves. (I have also seen inspired performers who, impressed with their original **Inspiration,** stopped their flow of creative excellence to self-congratulate and aggrandize.)

Matter lightens up when the spirit works on it. Think of yeast raising bread and ultra-light pumice rock filled with bubbles. Think of laughter and how it lightens a room, a good belly laugh that releases tension and opens our bodies to scoop up deep breaths.

One of the fastest routes of return to **Grace** is to laugh at yourself.

But laughing for no reason at all can get you there, too, as the physiological responses are the same. Christ the Healer has a "Laughter Coach" who comes to our Sunday Suppers and the Raw and Living Spirit Retreat. It doesn't take him long to get us going, and some of us start smiling as soon as he walks into the room.

When **Inspiration** adds energy to a human system, we are moved to be creative. New possibilities are opened, new ideas and experiences come, new potentials and powers are released.

The Holy Spirit brings gifts and fruits that are life renewing and world changing.

For the fruits of the Spirit are love, joy, peace, patience, kindness, gentleness, generosity, faithfulness and self-mastery. --Galatians 5

Have you ever been inspired by a great idea or a great person? What is it like to feel so alive and raring to go?

Bubbling Up
Dana Kelly Sweet

I once worked with a woman who was so severely agoraphobic that most days she couldn't bring herself to walk the twenty steps outside her door to her mailbox. Years of therapy had not erased the damage from a childhood of abuse and foster homes.

After showing her the **Triple Compass Map,** she told me that she had found a way to move from her inner hell of **Self Protection** to a state of **Grace** again.

Going to her computer, her window to the world, she would write a poem. Many of the poems were about her painful inner world, but the very process of writing them allowed **Inspiration** to take over and she was out of the pit.

> *Song sung blue weeping like a willow*
> *Song sung blue sleeping on my pillow*
> *Funny thing, but you can sing it with a cry in your voice*
> *And before you know, start to feeling good*
> *You simply got no choice*
> *--Neil Diamond*

Singing increases breathing and opens us to the grace of **Inspiration.**

Music in general can take us from one state of consciousness to another. A simple **Grace** practice is to identify songs that bring your consciousness up and sing them often, noticing your change of state. This also works to remove earworm songs like "You're So Vain" or "You Picked a Fine Time to Leave Me Lucille" that sometimes get stuck in my head like a **Self Protection** soundtrack.

Music can also be used in a drug like way, however, to induce trance states which can be a form of isolation or out of body experience, not embodied **Grace**. Notice the difference.

Gifted artists of all kinds play with **Inspiration.** You can probably recall many times when you were in the presence of inspired art, music, poetry, theater and more and were inspired, moved, ignited in your own creativity.

Scan your memories now for an outstanding example of being inspired and re-experience it in the present moment.

I'll never forget being in a large concert hall decades ago listening to Pete Seeger, the famed folksinger and activist. Onstage it was just Pete and his banjo, no fancy production or staging.

The air was electric as he passionately sang songs of justice, peace and freedom accompanied by a few quiet words of challenge to his young audience. Tears streamed in my eyes as I resonated with the pure humanizing effect he created by his simple presence.

Sobs and sighs open up locked down breathing much like laughter... Breathe. Just breathe.

****

Recipes in this chapter feature lively fermented foods, leavened with natural yeasts and bacteria that create healthful probiotics and sometimes fun bubbles. For yeast, like **Inspiration**, is in the air all around us, just waiting to get in and shake things up
.

Rejuvalac

Invented by Ann Wigmore, the apostle of wheat grass juice, rejuvalac is now unnecessarily out of favor with some raw groups due to inconsistent quality. Traditional recipes use gluten-containing grains such as wheat, kamut, rye, and barley. This blended quinoa version ferments faster resulting in fewer failures and also avoids the gluten.

Quinoa Rejuvalac

½ c organic quinoa seed, any color
filtered water

Rinse seeds and place in a nonmetal bowl or jar covered with fresh filtered water. Soak 4-8 hours, drain and rinse again. Allow to sprout 8-24 hrs. at room temperature. Rinse, and place in blender. Cover with water and blend for 5 seconds—no more. Pour into a gallon jar and fill to top with fresh filtered water. Cover with a clean cloth or nut milk bag and fasten with a rubber band. Let sit in a warm place. After 2 days, skim off any solids and taste. You can let it ferment 1 more day if it hasn't yet become pleasantly sour. Strain and bottle. Will stay fresh in fridge for up to 2 weeks. **Note:** if it smells rotten and stinky, pour it in the compost and try again.

Rejuvalac Infusions

After your rejuvalac is strained, you can add flavor by infusing the brew with any of the following: sliced fresh ginger, hot peppers, orange peel, lemongrass, and herbal tea bags. Simply add an ounce or less of any of these to a quart jar of pre-made rejuvalac, cover, and set out for a day, then strain and store in the fridge for up to a week.

Kefir

*Originally and still most commonly a dairy product, the two types of kefir grains can also be used to make vegan cultures. **Milk kefir** grains grow in dairy milk and look like tiny, gummy cauliflowers. They need to rest in cow or goat milk between vegan uses in order to thrive and reproduce. **Water kefir** grains are cubic-shaped and translucent like soft rock candy crystals and are happy to grow in sugar water alone, especially mineral laden spring water. Both types of grains, along with detailed instructions can be found on the internet. Single-use kefir packets which don't require a commitment to maintaining your own living cultures are also available.*

Almond Milk Kefir Fruit Smoothie

This is superior to yogurt drinks, with a tangy clean taste and a wider spectrum of probiotics. Drinking it daily helped us feel satisfied staying raw our first year. You can make it even more nutrient dense by adding a spoonful of bee pollen, which will then become more bio-available due to the probiotic bacteria breaking down the pollen coating. Nylon mesh nut milk bags can be homemade or purchased and work best for straining.

1 cup raw almonds, soaked 4-12 hours
1 cup raw cashews, soaked for 1 hour
1-2 active milk kefir grains
filtered water
2 ripe bananas and/or pears
1-2 pints fresh or frozen berries
2 peeled and seeded oranges

Rinse and drain soaked nuts. Place almonds in blender with 4 cups of fresh water and blend into a milk. Strain out pulp through a nut milk bag into a nonmetal bowl or jar. (Pulp will keep in the fridge for a few days or longer in the freezer and can be used in crackers and cakes as a raw flour.)

Remove your kefir grains from the dairy milk where they are growing and rinse them off gently with non-chlorinated water. Add rinsed kefir grains to the almond milk, cover, and keep in a warm place for 4-8 hours until the milk separates. Strain out the grains and culture them in fresh dairy milk until needed.

Put the kefired almond milk in the blender with the cashews, banana, orange, and berries and blend until smooth. Use within 2 days and keep refrigerated to slow down secondary fermentation.

Kefir Hazelnut Nog

A comforting party drink or just breakfast, this out-competes dairy eggnog on flavor as well as healthfulness.

4 cups fresh hazelnut milk
2 milk kefir grains, rinsed in non-chlorinated water
2 ripe bananas or pears, chopped
1 t cinnamon
1 t vanilla
 sprinkle of nutmeg

First make hazelnut milk using almond milk procedure above. Culture the hazelnut milk for 8-12 hours with the milk kefir grains in a warm place. Remove grains and culture them in fresh dairy milk until needed. Return hazelnut kefir to blender and add remaining ingredients except nutmeg. Blend until smooth. Serve gently warm in pre-warmed cups with a sprinkle of nutmeg on top.

Cashew-Hemp Creamy Cheese

Once your milk kefir "farm" is reproducing, you can spare a grain to make this delicious spread or dip. Try it on a piece of onion bread topped with some marinated tomatoes and olives. You can also culture this cheese with a probiotic capsule if you don't have the kefir grains available.

2 cups raw cashews or 1 cup each raw cashews and brazil nuts
½ cup hemp seed
½-1 t unprocessed salt
1 small milk kefir grain or probiotic capsule
filtered water

Soak the nuts for 1 hour (do not over-soak) and drain. Place in blender with the rest of the ingredients and cover with water. Blend until smooth and pour into a non-metal container. Cover and leave at room temperature for 12-24 hours, then refrigerate. It is ready at this point, but will continue to ripen and thicken for a few more days. Keeps about a week in the fridge.

Coconut Water Kefir

The water from young Thai-type coconuts is already fantastically healthful, and adding the kefir probiotics makes it more so. Most groceries serving Asian people carry these immature coconuts (not the brown ones) in their distinctive shaved white husks. You can open them easily with a strong knife or cleaver. Good how-to videos can be found on YouTube. Be sure to enjoy the pulp after you've strained out the precious liquid for this sparkling drink.

water from 2 young coconuts
1-2 T water kefir crystals (or 1 probiotic capsule)

Gently rinse your water kefir grains in non-chlorinated water. Gently stir kefir or the contents of the opened probiotic capsule into the coconut water in a non-metallic container, cover, and keep in a warm place. Depending on warmth, it can be ready in 4-24 hours. When tangy but still fresh tasting, strain out the grains and return them to fresh sugar water to continue growing. Do not over-culture your drink or it will taste too sour and be a waste of good coconuts.

Grape Kefir Sangria

This sangria and the Sparkling Apple Cider below are two clever ways to re-vivify pasteurized fruit juices by culturing them with water kefir crystals. Of course, it is always preferable to start with fresh squeezed juices if you can. The more sugar in your fruit juice, the more alcohol will be produced over time, so drink these within a day or take the consequences.

½ gallon pure grape juice, any type
2-4 T water kefir grains (also called crystals)
2 organic oranges, one juiced, the other sliced
juice of 1 lemon or lime
4 c watermelon, juiced or blended

Strain your grains and rinse gently in non-chlorinated water. Stir into grape juice and cover lightly. Culture in a warm place for 4-24 hours. Strain out grains and replace in fresh sugar water in the fridge to preserve for future use. Refrigerate grape kefir. Will continue secondary fermentation until all sugar is used up, becoming "drier" and more alcoholic. To make sangria, mix in fruits and juices just before serving.

Sparkling Apple Cider

You can try this same procedure with any 100% fruit juice with varying results. This one is always good.

½ gallon apple cider
2-4 T water kefir grains
Combine the grains with the apple cider in a nonmetallic jar and cover loosely for gases to escape. It helps to leave a little room at the top, too. Culture 12-24 hours to your taste. Strain out grains and replace them in fresh sugar water in the fridge to preserve for future use. Refrigerate the sparkling apple cider until needed. Will continue to keep with some secondary fermentation in the refrigerator for several weeks.

Ginger Beer

*This is the basic procedure for making water kefir with sugar, fruit and spices. You can try it with whatever strikes your fancy. We particularly like **Orange-Chocolate Mint Water Kefir** with the peel of an organic orange and a large bunch of chocolate mint in the culture. Strong tasting sugars like Rapadura will dominate the flavor, but provide more minerals and keep your cultures healthier. Always strain out the grains from your cultures before 24 hours, usually 12-18 is about right, when it tastes the best.*

1 gallon filtered water
½ – 1 c water kefir grains
1 c sugar, any type
½ cup sliced fresh ginger
optional: peel of ½ an organic orange

Combine grains with sugar, water, and ginger slices in a gallon jar. Cover lightly and set in a warm place to culture for 12-24 hours. Strain out grains, discard ginger, bottle and refrigerate up to 2 weeks until needed.

Water Kefir Variations

Here's some more combinations I like to add to the sugar water/kefir brew: organic lemon peel with fennel seeds, mint leaves with orange peel, raisins and fresh tarragon, chopped vanilla bean and dried coconut.

Pickling Procedures

Fear not, making lacto-fermented pickles is as old as the hills. It's also easier than finding unpasteurized pickle products, because most of what passes for store bought pickles are made with vinegar, skipping the live fermentation process, where beneficial lacto bacteria create the acidic environment that preserves food without canning or refrigeration. Basically, you just pack your canning jar or crock with veggies, cover them with a brine solution and leave them somewhere to ferment for a few days. You'll need a clean non-metallic container, your chosen vegetables, filtered water, and good (unprocessed) salt. Sufficient salt discourages bad bacteria until the good ones produce enough lactic acid. You can speed the fermentation by adding the contents of a probiotic capsule if you wish. Pickling time varies by ambient temperature, taste and vegetable. Many recipes and variations are available. Here's a few to try.

Pink Sauerkraut

Sauerkraut is created from pounding shredded cabbage in layers with salt sprinkled between to release the liquid and create the brine. This recipe will fill up a gallon jar after pounding.

2 fresh green cabbages
1 fresh red cabbage
4 T unprocessed salt

Shred cabbage thinly with a knife, mandoline or 2 mm food processor slicing blade.

Save a couple leaves to cover the top. Put several cups of shredded cabbage in the jar, sprinkle with some of the salt, and pound down vigorously with a clean heavy stick or rolling pin end (the kind that doesn't have a handle) until liquid is expressed. Continue until jar is full and all of the salt is used. Press reserved leaves over the mixture to cover. Add filtered water if needed to bring brine level up to the top. Fill a strong quart-sized Ziploc bag with water and place over the jar opening to weight and seal out air. Place jar in a drip pan in a warm place and leave to culture 2-7 days, depending on how sour you like it.

Pickled Beets

Clean, peel, and cut enough beets to fill your container. Add 1 T salt (not iodized) per quart and water to within ½ inch of the top. Cover and set in a larger bowl to capture any leaking brine. Should be ready to eat after about 3 days in a warm place, or leave out a bit longer until pleasantly sour. Will keep in a cool dark place for several months or much longer in the fridge.

Curtido

A kind of Latin American sauerkraut with carrots and onions. This is the traditional way to make it, not the common vinegar-based pickle that may garnish your plate at a Mexican restaurant.

1 large green cabbage, shredded
2 c carrots, grated
1 c onions, sliced thin
1 T dried oregano
½ t red pepper flakes
2 T unprocessed salt

Mix ingredients together in a large bowl. Pound with a wooden pounder until juices are released. Pack into 2 quart-sized mason jars and press down until juices cover cabbage. Leave an inch of space at the top, cover tightly and keep at room temperature for about 3 days before storing in a cool dark place or the fridge.

Milk and water Kefir grains, Rejuvalac, Pink Sauerkraut, Curtido

Chapter 5

Awe/Wonder

There are only two ways to live your life. One is as though nothing is a miracle. The other is as if everything is. --Albert Einstein

Everyone was filled with awe,
and many wonders and miraculous signs
were done by the apostles. –Acts 2:43

Inspiration fermenting and bubbling within us may expand to the point where we burst into **Awe.**

Awe, or wonder, is the fifth named **Grace** on our **Compass.**

In many English translations of the Bible, it is mistranslated as fear, as in the "fear of the Lord." But they are so different. Fear causes us to flinch and contract, to shy away and hide.

Awe brings us to a greater sense of the self we thought we knew and the world we assumed we understood.

Many people in our workshops recall moments of being awestruck in nature.

Scan your memory for such treasured times you've filed away and lost track of. Be there now. Where are you? What is around you? How do you feel? Can you speak or move?

The tallest waterfall here in Oregon is called Multnomah Falls, plunging 620 feet down over a set of cliffs right next to Interstate 84 as it winds through the magnificent Columbia Gorge.

A walking bridge connects the trail that bisects the falls. Every day, thousands of tourists and many wedding parties stop on that waterfall-misted bridge for photos.

When I stop by, I like to stand right in the middle of the bridge, turn my back to the thundering water, raise my arms to catch the spray and imagine what it's like to meld into that great cataract. Later, when I turn to face the erupting white curtain, I am hypnotized by crashing cascades, terribly tempted to dive in and ride them to the boiling pit below.

Once I visited the falls when they were even more wondrous. It was winter and the swollen river of falling water shot heavier and louder than my eyes and ears could almost bear standing so close on the bridge.

But we had also had an unusually frigid week of temperatures in the teens.

The mist had frozen in fractal patterns all over the rock face and surrounding trees. Entranced, I gazed at a fairyland of icy stalagmites and stalactites covering the landscape and littering the snowy, frozen surface of the pool far below me with piles of crystal shards. Underneath the ice curtaining the falls I could still see the water flowing down like molten taffy.

Awe in the presence of immensity gave rise to classical forms of worship. In a majestic vision, the prophet Isaiah, caught up in an experience of Deity in the temple in Jerusalem, fell on his face in **Awe.**

I saw the LORD seated on a throne and the train of his robe filled the temple. Above him were seraphs...and they were calling to one another:

> *'Holy, holy, holy is the LORD Almighty; the whole earth is full of his glory.'*
> *---Isaiah 6:2-4*

Contemplating Totality, either as unimaginable vastness, void, or infinitely small can quickly instill a sense of **Awe.**

All someone has to do in one of our workshops is describe a wondrous encounter with nature and the rest of us feel like we are lifted up with them. In **Awe,** we identify not as our small selves but with our essence a reflection of the great I AM.

What is the body memory of **Awe** for you? The posture, the breathing? The sounds coming out of your mouth or the dumbstruck silence? Remember; be there now.

Wow
Dana Kelly Sweet

Late one fall, Thomas and I were driving home from a trip to California up coastal Highway 1. It almost sunset, but I wanted to walk through redwoods, so we pulled into the empty parking lot of the Lady Bird Johnson Grove which offered a well-marked trail. Plunging into the woods, we were almost immediately confronted with a grandfather tree so large that a whole family of humans hugging it together couldn't get their arms around its girth. It was so still, you could hear the mushrooms growing.

Golden light filtered through the ancient forest as we climbed a small rise where the setting sun mixing with evening mist burned like red fire and smoke behind those massive trees set like standing stones in a sacred grove. "Aah. Aaah. Aaaah," was all I could say, feeling staggered by the beauty. "Aah! I, uh, think I have a new reference for **Awe.**"

Through practice, I have learned something useful about the grace of **Awe:** it can grow.

Formerly, I equated **Awe** with overwhelm, with senses on full tilt, unable to take in any more. But after finding **Awe** in my body memory and bringing it forward in a daily meditation over a number of weeks, I discovered that my capacity to hold **Awe** as a physical experience expanded. It's like exercising an **Awe**-muscle. The breakdown at limit of capacity allows a stronger muscle to form. And a richer one.

Now I can appreciate the subtler, quieter nuances of wonder that I missed before. Which means I can know more and more **Awe.**

Which seems like a good capacity to stretch if you are intending to live in the kin- dom of heaven now.

Here is a surprising but effective way Thomas and I use the key of **Awe** to unlock ourselves from a state of **Self Protection** and return to **Grace:** to be in **Awe** of our own massive foolishness.

For we humans are each given the freedom to create and elaborate our personal psychological universe by telling stories that make meaning of our sensory experiences.

So from what is nearly always simply a difference of perception, we imagine scenarios about ourselves and others filled with hurt, threat, resentment, disappointment, aversion, isolation and other terrors and impose these as our "reality" on God's creation.

It's **Awe**-inspiring in its own way for me to recognize how I can ruin a perfectly beautiful summer day by dwelling in self pity or on the story of some past loss. Or what a colossal mess I can make of trying and failing to get along in certain relationships, what amazing Gordian knots I can tangle myself up in psychologically.

In my self-created universe of feelings, the bummer I can generate and maintain is truly awesome! Realizing that, Thomas and I can laugh at ourselves and move out of our misery from there into any **Grace.**

****

So what recipes can we associate with **Awe**? How about foods that are "over the top"?

Once at Sunday Supper we served a white chocolate raspberry cheesecake and the whole room got quiet as we savored each bite.

Given our alive palates and high energy levels, raw foodist creativity restlessly ranges the globe for new and more wonderful taste sensations as well as foods and condiments that promise even more vitality and rejuvenation.

Not far behind the chefs, entrepreneurs package and distribute these wonders as "superfoods". The list of so-called raw superfoods is long and growing, including exotic (for Northern hemisphere folk at least) fruits like durian, lucuma, acai, golden (Inca) berry, goji or wolfberry; nutrition boosters like algae, spirulina and plankton; medicinal mushrooms and herbs; and indigenous seeds and vegetables like chia and maca.

Number one on the list, of course, is raw cacao, though it relative virtues and vices are warmly debated among raw foodists. To this I would add the humbler but nutrition-packed carob in its raw flour form.

So here are some of our favorite carob and chocolate recipes, along with a sampler including some of the other superfoods available through raw food sellers on the internet.

Carob Honey Mint Taffy

An older name for carob is St. John's bread, a reference to it being the food of John the Baptist, who was said to eat "honey and locust." According to Leviticus 11:22, John could have been eating kosher grasshoppers, but most agree that John was actually eating the fruit of the locust tree, the carob pod. I usually make this treat during Advent to celebrate John's life of preparing the way for Christ.

2 T raw honey
1 c carob flour
2 drops peppermint essential oil or ¼ t extract
walnut halves, optional

Mix and knead by hand until all the flour is incorporated. It will seem dry until it magically takes on a taffy-like consistency. Then roll into small balls and refrigerate. For presentation, press the balls into walnut halves.

Carob Fudge

1 c carob flour
2 c pitted medjool dates
½ c coconut oil
1 c shredded coconut
2 t vanilla

Blend ingredients together in a food processor or by hand, press into a flat shape and cut.

Refrigerator Brownies

I make these soft, quick to prepare brownies whenever I have leftover almond pulp and people to feed.

1 c almond pulp
1 ½ c raisins
2 T raw honey, coconut nectar, dates, or agave syrup
1 T extra virgin coconut oil
1 t vanilla
½ t cinnamon
sprinkle of unprocessed salt
5 T carob and/or cacao powder in any proportion
1 c walnuts

optional: ½ c cacao nibs
variation: Blend in a small bunch of fresh chocolate mint.

Puree almond pulp with raisins in a food processor until raisins are broken up and mixed in. Pulse in remaining ingredients until mixed. Place on plate and shape into a rectangle about ½" thick. Cut into small brownies, chill, and serve.

Chocolate Kefir Smoothie/Parfait

Thomas created this rich variation of almond milk kefir. For a dazzling dessert, layer with banana chunks and fresh berries.

2 c prepared almond milk kefir (see recipe in **Inspiration** chapter, page 62)
2 ripe bananas or pears
1 c raisins
½ c cacao nibs
1 vanilla bean
1 c cashews
¼ c extra virgin coconut oil
sprinkle of unprocessed salt

Put everything in a blender and blend for several minutes until smooth. Chill to thicken before using as a parfait. Use within 2 days as secondary fermentation continues even under refrigeration.

Chocolate Bark and Bites

Raw foodists can be funny. We delight in superior food, but then sometimes indulge in raw chocolate, whose health benefits are debatable at best. You'll understand why if you try this.

½ lb. raw cacao butter
½ c raw agave syrup or Coconut Nectar (more or less, to taste)
½ c raw cacao powder
2 T maca powder
½ c each raisins, dried goji berries, cashew pieces and macadamia nuts
1 t vanilla
½ t unprocessed salt

Melt the cacao butter in a small metal bowl placed in a bowl of hot water. When the butter has liquefied, stir in the rest of the ingredients. Pour into a shallow container and place in freezer for about 15 minutes to harden. Break into pieces to share.

Rocky Road Cream Ice

Whips up gratifyingly fast in your food processor. Tastes and feels so good to eat you won't miss the mini marshmallows.

½ c almonds
2 frozen bananas
meat of 2 frozen avocados
¼ c raw cacao or carob powder
1 T honey, coconut nectar or agave nectar
1 t vanilla

Chop the almonds roughly by pulsing them a few times in the food processor, then set aside. Cut the bananas and avocados into smallish chunks with a knife, then pulse in food processor with the cacao, sweetener and vanilla until blended but still frozen. Mix in almonds. Serve immediately or put in freezer for a few minutes to firm up if needed before serving.

Mint Chip Cream Ice

Replace the almonds in the above recipe with ½ c cacao nibs and ½ t peppermint extract or 2 drops peppermint essential oil for a refreshing treat.

Fear No Chocolate

My husband developed this in the early days of raw chocolate when only cacao nibs and not powder were available. We still make it in quantity for fairs and parties, where it is quite popular. The lemon peel is the secret and essential ingredient for its bright flavor.

½ cup cacao nibs ground in coffee or spice grinder
½ cup raw carob flour
1/2 cup raw coconut butter
¼-½ cup raw coconut nectar, agave nectar or honey
peel of 2 organic lemons, finely diced
8 cups (approx.) dried shredded coconut

Thoroughly mix all ingredients except dried coconut by hand or in a food processor. Place in a large bowl and work in coconut until it can be rolled into small balls. The amount of coconut depends on how much sweetener you use, as its stickiness, with the coconut butter, is what holds the balls together. Chill.

Durian-Avo smoothie

Inspired by an artificially flavored and sweetened version we came across at an Asian market, which is where you find the exotic spiky oversized football durians, along with the young Thai coconuts. Thomas says he can't describe the truly exotic flavor, but he loves it. Nutrient dense, with the full complement of essential amino acids and good fats, share this treat with friends who wonder where you get your protein.

1 c durian pulp (can still be a bit frozen)
1 avocado, peeled and seeded
water and meat of 1 young Thai coconut (less or more depending on thickness desired)

optional: ½ t spirulina or algae powder for color and extra nutrition
Put everything together in a blender and blend until smooth.

Green Superjuice

Juicing is the fastest way to get vitamins and minerals into your system short of a blood transfusion, as it removes most of the fiber which slows down digestion and absorption. Fiber is of course necessary and good for us. Juices are not whole foods, so I consider juicing a therapeutic activity or a tonic. If you make a low-glycemic vegetable juice with wild greens—nature's true superfoods—you can probably cure almost anything. What you can juice will depend on your equipment. Some juicers handle greens better than others. If you want this powerful fluid to be palatable, go easy on the strongly flavored vegetables.

Prepare vegetables for your juicer. Include some roots like **beet, carrot, Jerusalem artichoke, parsnip, burdock, turmeric, turnip, radish, rutabaga, yacon;** low glycemic fruits like **tomato, sweet and hot peppers, cucumber, apple, berries, bitter melon, watermelon rind, squashes;** and leaves like **celery, kale, collard, bok choy, cabbage, chard, aloe, fresh or rehydrated seaweeds, parsley, sprouts, wheatgrass, cilantro, nettles, dandelion, purslane or other seasonal weeds.** You can also add cut up organic lemon with the peel, a clove of **garlic** or some fresh **ginger.**

Elemental Chia

Easy, not fancy or pretty, and blandly satisfying like the Cream of Wheat of my childhood. Aztec warriors are said to have thrived on this mush during long cross country trips. Chia seeds are still convenient to pack along when you are traveling. You could make a nicer breakfast of it by stirring in some thick almond milk and berries, or using a mashed ripe banana in place of the water.

½ c chia seeds, white or black
1 c filtered water

Mix seeds and water together in a bowl, stirring to break up lumps. Mixture will congeal to a thick paste in a few minutes and be ready to eat.

Superfood Trail Mix

Take this with you in your backpack, suitcase or back seat when you travel. You will not lose weight or feel too sorry for yourself away from your gourmet raw kitchen, I promise. And if you are also able to confect green smoothies on the road, you will still have a healthy and satisfying eating experience.

Combine dried goji berries, Inca berries (aka golden berrries), raisins, cacao nibs, hulled sunflower seeds, pumpkin seeds, walnuts, almonds, brazil nuts and/or cashews in a bowl and mix well

Chocolate Kefir with Chocolate Bark and Bites

Chapter 6

Peace

Dona Nobis Pacem (Give us your peace)
--Latin chant

Give peace a chance
—John Lennon

Why is peace so hard for us humans? Prayers for peace have risen to heaven ceaselessly throughout history to this very day.

Despite universal longing, mostly it seems we humans only find a measure of **Peace** after bitter struggle, harmony through conflict. **Peace** at last. Too often it comes in battlefield strewn with silent dead. Or to loved ones embracing, exhausted, wordless, after a vicious fight.

Maybe we only find it after "losing it all" (fill in the blank), hitting bottom, surrendering our pride and accepting that we are powerless to control life. And then feel oddly at **Peace** for the first time.

Peace
Dana Kelly Sweet

Why is **Peace** so hard to achieve? Perhaps the question is the key. **Peace** is not achieved. It is a given.

Peace simply *is*, but humans in body believe we have to struggle with others and the world around us to be safe, to be free, to be fulfilled, to be worthy, to be who we are, to belong.

Peace I leave with you. My peace I give you. I do not give to you as the world gives. Do not let your hearts be troubled and do not be afraid. --John 14:27

Shalom, or **Peace** in its biblical meaning, is much more than the absence of conflict.

It is positive reconciliation, at-one-ment with all beings. A state of **Grace** where we may choose to stand—or not. Only our inner resistance can stop us from being at *Peace.*

We are perfectly capable of making the shift in our consciousness to see the world with the eyes of **Peace** instead of imagining, creating and defending ourselves against enemies all around.

Blessed are the peacemakers, for theirs is the kingdom of heaven---Matthew 5:9

We may recognize and seek **Peace** in two basic forms: inner and outer.

Many of us have discovered the hard way that they go together and inner **Peace** comes first. Otherwise, internally divided, believing in separation, and imagining enemies, we will find even tit for tat mutuality impossible to sustain.

Conflicted, unhappy people sow chaos all around no matter what mask they present to the world. An angry parent fails to pacify a child. And whatever its short term gains, a violent peace movement can never succeed. We must *be* **Peace** to make **Peace.**

In the event of an emergency, oxygen masks will drop from the compartments above your seat. Please adjust your own mask before attempting to assist others.

While better than open warfare, forms of mutuality such as equality (as measured against some debated standard), a balance of power, negotiated compromise, cease-fires, etc, are at best conflict management strategies and at worst Mutually Assured Destruction.

However far away it may seem in any given situation, surely there is some time we each have tasted the **Grace** of **Peace**. True **Peace** so powerful it can endure calmly in the midst of chaos, like the eye of a hurricane.

There are moments in our memories when we truly felt peaceful. Or can imagine it.

Be there now. What are the circumstances where you find yourself at **Peace?**

How old are you? Are you alone or with others? Are you sitting, standing, or lying down?

Some experience the period of transitioning from wakefulness to sleep a daily time of **Peace.** Whatever peaceful moment you find, inhabit it as a full body memory of **Peace**. Color in as much of the scene and action as possible.

Breathe. Are you breathing?
Deliberately slowing one's breathing is an effective way to begin shifting out of emotional reactivity into a calmer state. Vietnamese Buddhist monk Thich Nat Han suggests simply imagining **Peace** as you breathe in and out. Physically, this exercise will lower your blood pressure and allow your body to clean out the fight or flight hormone dump in your bloodstream.

Breathe. Just breathe.

What else helps you shift into a state of **Peace**?

I like to walk along the ocean's edge when I'm upset, gaze into the flames of a fire, lean into a wild wind or stand by a river and let it all wash away.

Giving or receiving Reiki may fill a body and the room with **Peace.** A good massage can release the stress and tension we hold in our muscles and fascia.

We can also touch **Peace** by actively remembering or imagining these things present.

Sweet **Peace** may come to us after being struck with **Awe** when the veil parts to let the big picture reveal itself for a moment. Then there is nothing to do, nothing to say.

After a sublime mystical experience, the great doctor of the medieval church, St. Thomas Aquinas, announced that all he had written, including his masterwork *Summa Theologica*, now seemed like so much straw.

Terrified by his success at calling signs and wonders to testify against the corrupt government, the prophet Elijah ran for his life to Mt. Sinai and hid in a cave.

Outside, God called in an earthquake, a mighty wind and a raging fire. Elijah stayed hunkered down because it was just too much.

But then it got quiet and he heard God in the silence, emerging in wonder at the "still, small voice" of **Peace.**

> *The peace of God, which transcends all understanding---Philippians 4:7*

Peace is just about Jesus' favorite word. Imagine that you can feel his breath, hear him saying, "**Peace** be with you," and let yourself really receive God's **Peace** as a gift beyond understanding.

Allow yourself to extend the gift to be at **Peace** not only with God, but also with your neighbors and yourself. Extend **Peace** with your imagination to your whole life: present, past, and future.

Can you think of a better way to be prepared for uncertain times ahead than cultivating an awareness of **Peace**? Our church members support one another in welcoming drastic life changes by singing this little chant in our prayer circle:

> *Doors closing, doors opening*
> *Doors closing, doors I'm opening*
> *I am safe, it's only change*
> *I am safe, it's only change*
> *(author unknown)*

We can each shift from emotional turmoil to **Peace** by asking ourselves, "What's the worst that can happen?" and face it down.

No matter what it is, you know you are still OK if you will trust the higher truth you intuitively know is real.

If that feels impossible, as it often does, the Work of Byron Katie offers several other useful questions. These can help create a little wedge of doubt—a "thalamic pause" that refreshes—in an emotionally charged story: "Is it true? Can I absolutely be sure that it is true?"

Looking back, we may find the crisis was necessary to break through our ego's strangling grasp to save the small self at all costs.

Higher wisdom says we must let go and lose our lives to save them, to experience the abundant, everlasting life of oneness with the greater Self.

This is difficult to achieve because you must first *have* a life to lose it. Only individuated persons can freely make the sacrifice of ceasing to insist on their personal self-importance and give their self-created "life" away.

In **Peace,** individual distinctions recede into the background, making their contribution but not needing to call attention to themselves.

There is a sublime selflessness to **Peace**. It is like waking on a winter morning to snow covering the landscape, harmonizing the forms into a beautiful, quiet tableau.

****

Our recipes for **Peace** in this chapter include soups and stews where the flavors blend and harmonize. Most are prepared only by chopping and blending, so they are ready in a flash. **Peace** now.

Andy's Not Split Pea Soup

Brings back the memories, but nary a boiled pea or bacon bit in sight. Invented by our friend and popular Sunday Supper chef Andy Williams.

2 c winter squash, peeled, seeded and chopped
1 c carrot, chopped
1 c sprouted lentils
¼ c sun dried tomatoes
½ bunch spinach
2 c filtered water
1 t each onion powder, cumin powder, thyme and basil
½ t garlic powder
unprocessed salt and fresh black pepper to taste
2 pitted dates, optional

To mimic a split pea soup texture, first pulse the lentils in a food processor briefly, sprinkle with salt and set aside to marinate for an 1-8 hours, refrigerated. Soak the tomatoes in the water for an hour, then combine everything in a blender but the lentils and blend until smooth. Adjust seasonings. Stir in the macerated lentils and serve.

Traveling Mercies Soup

This was another traveling success story, but it takes pre-planning.

Cut and dry **leeks, parsley, mushrooms, celery, tomatoes, squash, red pepper,** etc., when they are in season and store in sealed jars out of the light. When you are packing for your trip, powder what you plan to use in a Vitamix or coffee grinder. Add salt and pepper to taste and package securely.

Also pack a sprouting bag, soaking container, and fast sprouting seeds such as **sunflower, mung beans, lentils, radish,** and **alfalfa.** At your destination, soak seeds overnight. Pour into bag, rinse and hang or prop on your container near the sink if possible. To use, pour a couple tablespoons in a cup, add warm water and stir. Wait a minute and stir in sprouts. Leave a nice tip for the housekeeper if you are doing this in a hotel.

Andy's Corn Chowder

If we are nice to Andy, he will make this for Sunday Supper. Rich with cashews and mushrooms and fresh corn, there's never any leftovers.

1 large head broccoli
1 lb. cherry tomatoes
3 lb. white button mushrooms
½ lb. cashews
Kernels cut from 6 ears of corn
1 lb. carrots, juiced
1 c filtered water
2 T extra virgin olive oil
2 T Coconut Aminos
1 t unprocessed salt
1 large red bell pepper
½ t white pepper
2 T onion powder
1 t oregano
pinch cayenne

Chop broccoli, slice tomatoes and mushrooms. Place all in a large bowl and add 1 t salt. Massage well, then dehydrate for 6-8 hours until soft. Blend remaining ingredients together until smooth, reserving 1 c of corn. Combine everything in a large bowl when the first three ingredients are done.

Butternut Nut Soup

A mild tasting, easy soup that goes well with crackers and a salad.

1 medium butternut squash or equivalent, peeled, seeded and chopped
1 c of soaked raw almonds or hazelnuts
1 bunch celery
1 medium shallot
1 T each fresh sage and thyme, chopped, or 2 t poultry seasoning
unprocessed salt and pepper to taste.
    2-4 c filtered water

Put ingredients in a blender. Use more or less water depending on thickness and richness desired.

Savory Green Smoothie Soup

Recently we were traveling with our blender so we could make green smoothies for breakfast on the road. After stopping at a farmer's market, we made this tasty soup for dinner, too. Vegetables and herbs can be varied, but the basic "stock" is the tomatoes. Alive with flavor, no salt is needed.

4 ripe tomatoes, chopped
1-2 colored bell peppers, seeded
½ jalapeno, optional
 juice of 1 lemon
1 clove of garlic or a small onion
1 cucumber or zucchini
1 carrot, chopped
1 bunch cilantro or spinach, washed and chopped
1 avocado, peeled and seeded
2-3 cups filtered water

 Blend everything together to desired texture.

Celery Root Soup

Fresh raw soups don't get much easier or tastier than this. It's a good reason to grow or get acquainted with this surprisingly—judging from appearances— mellow root vegetable.

 2 c celeriac, (also known as celery root) peeled and chopped
 4 c filtered water
 ¼ c fresh lemon juice
 unprocessed salt and fresh ground black pepper to taste

Blend everything together and serve.

Marvelous Miso Soup

Raw kelp noodles are a great new product you may have to look for. You can still make this soup without them, though. Miso is a living food, fermented and aged bean paste with many health benefits. It is available at Asian groceries and health food stores and keeps a long time in its container in the refrigerator, so I always have it around. I make this soup when the weather gets cold and serve it warm into pre-warmed bowls.

4 c filtered water
6 T miso
1 finely minced garlic clove
2 t finely minced ginger
1 small bunch green onions, chopped
½ package kelp noodles or 1/4 c alternate sea vegetable
1 c bean sprouts
2 c very finely sliced (best to use a mandoline) mixed vegetables, including carrots, celery, red pepper, cabbage, Asian greens
½ c thin sliced shitake mushrooms
¼ c Coconut Aminos (another new raw product) or Nama Shoyu

Warm the water and stir in the miso until it is dissolved. Add the other ingredients except for the noodles. Keep warm for about a half hour to allow vegetables to soften. Stir in noodles and re-warm a few minutes before serving in ceramic bowls warmed in hot water or an oven.

Mango Salsa Soup

This could begin its life as a salsa for lunch and then blend into a first course soup for supper.

4 red bell peppers, seeded and chopped
2 ripe mangoes, peeled, seeded and chopped
1 bunch cilantro
juice of 2 limes
½ jalapeno, seeded and chopped
½ t unprocessed salt

Put everything together in a blender and blend until smooth.

Holiday Spice Dessert Soup
Smells as good as it tastes.

4 c fresh squeezed orange juice
2 c chopped carrots
2 pitted dates
1 c macadamia, Brazils, cashews or some combination, soaked for 1 hour
1 t cinnamon
½ t each ginger powder, cardamom and cloves
pinch of salt
raisins or pomegranate seeds for garnish

Combine ingredients and blend until smooth and creamy. Serve in small bowls with a few raisins or pomegranate seeds sprinkled on top.

Strawberry Gazpacho

6 cups organic strawberries, hulled
2 large cucumbers, peeled and chopped
½ c sweet onion, peeled and chopped
1 c filtered water
2 T raw apple cider vinegar
1 c loose packed basil, washed and de-stemmed
2 T extra virgin olive oil
½ t unprocessed salt
 black pepper, cayenne and/or fresh jalapeno to taste

Blend until smooth. Taste for seasonings and serve chilled or at room temperature.

Watermelon Gazpacho
Another refreshing take on an old summer standard.

2 c tomatoes, chopped
1 cucumber, chopped
4 c watermelon, chopped (don't remove seeds, they are good for you)
small bunch of basil—holy basil is especially good with watermelon
unprocessed salt and fresh ground black pepper to taste

Put everything in the blender and pulse until mixed but not totally pureed.

Watermelon Fruit Soup

Fruit soups are a traditional first course in some cultures. A good idea that could spread.

4 c watermelon, chopped
2 pints fresh blackberries
juice of 1 lime

Put everything together in a blender and blend until smooth.

Melon Seed and Fruit Soup

There's something extra in this soup—the goodness and flavor of the seeds.

1 ripe cantaloupe or other melon, peeled and chopped—reserve seeds
juice of 1 lemon or lime
nutmeg
1 c filtered water

Scoop out the cantaloupe seeds and place in blender with water. Blend for about a minute and then strain through a nut milk bag. Discard pulp. Return strained liquid to blender, add fruit and lemon juice, re-blend and serve.

Marvelous Miso Soup

Chapter 7

Presence

God was in Christ, reconciling the world.
--2 Corinthians 5:19

Have you ever stopped to contemplate the miracle of simply being alive?

...Of your **Presence** here, self-aware as a being in a body that is able to interact with other bodies   and a physical environment?

...Of having senses to appreciate what you encounter in the environment and something called time to mark the changes in the life around and within you, even if it sometimes feels like being in a bind?

...Of being equipped with a human operating system as unique as any snowflake to drive around   and explore life with?

Leaving the question of how we each happened to be here on earth to the theologians, let us focus on the fact that we experience ourselves, including our emotions and thoughts, through the medium of a body, and yet also have the sense that we are more than that.

It seems that we are also an awareness, sometimes called a soul, that isn't limited by physical constraints.

We are, as Christ was said to be, incarnate—literally, "in meat bodies"—essential human being-ness having the experience of being embodied and interacting with other bodies.

The miracle of embodiment is what allows us to feel and act as though we were separate, yet it need not keep us from knowing that we are not limited to the physical.

To see the world in a grain of sand,
and heaven in a wild flower

To hold infinity in the palm of your hand
and eternity in an hour

--William Blake

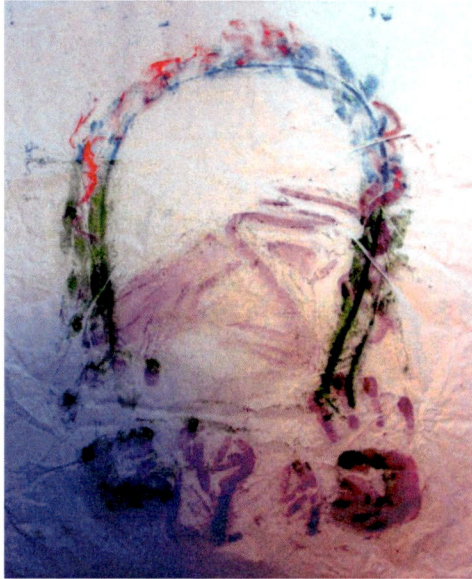

Go There
Dana Kelly Sweet

Think of the great sacrifice a human being makes to be born into this earthly world from the realm of spirit.

We leave the company of angels basking before the face of God to take on the constrictions of time and space and heavy material density. Awareness of our divine origin and destiny becomes cloaked away from us.

Animal survival instincts and drives come hardwired into our flesh, creating a barrage of information streaming to our senses indicating that we are alone and vulnerable.

Our reaction to the shock of birth and the painful trauma of felt separation from Oneness leads to a struggle for survival and control, setting us on our particular path on the **Compass of Getting Along**.

We develop and refine numerous physical, mental, and emotional coping mechanisms in a futile effort to feel more secure. This struggle can preoccupy us for a lifetime, completely occluding awareness of any higher truth or human potential.

The coping habits we develop may become unconscious over time or so familiar and obvious to us that they are unquestioned "second nature."

Yet inexorably, they create distortions in our physique that eventually show up as accelerated aging and illness.
These in turn, we may choose to fear, condemn, and resist, causing us to feel more vulnerable and tempted to hunker down into the isolation of the *Compass of Self Protection* when this world gives us the painful message that we don't belong here.

As a consequence, many of us are not fully **Present** in our bodies much of the time. We simply don't notice or register most of what's coming at us or going on around us.

Into this painfully recurring situation, as the Christian story goes, comes another being of divine origin, volunteering as we each do, to take on the dreadful limitations of physical existence.

The difference is that even in "the body of a slave" as the Bible puts it, Jesus absolutely knew and remembered the wider truth of being human.

He dedicates his life to teaching and demonstrating that truth as the gospel of the kin-dom of God on earth as it is in heaven.

There are even moments on record when his veil of flesh becomes transparent to reveal the mystery of human *metamorphosis* (transfiguration) and resurrection.

His life is a gift to the species, a template of how to be fully, spiritually, humanly *alive* in flesh.

We can choose to access his template to follow him.

But first we have to stop hating our physicality, running from our pain, living in our imaginations, and instead choose to be **Present** in our God given bodies here and now.

Take this moment to notice how you are holding your body. How you are breathing. Where any tension is located, any discomfort or pain.

Lovingly, gently breathe into where it hurts. Open your heart to this body of yours. Remember what it feels like to be grateful. Forgive yourself for damaging your body and then compounding the damage by hating it.

Have you noticed how small postural distortions become exaggerated with age?

Many bodies whose owners have enjoyed a lifetime of ease actually look beaten down by the years, hold tremendous rigidity and tension, are collapsed inward, or are bent over as though dragging impossibly heavy burdens.

The cause of this accumulated physical damage is mostly psychological, if unconscious.

Thankfully, the seeds of our healing as well as our self destruction are held in our bodies. Pain and dysfunction may get our attention and set us on a search for real cure that can take us far beyond standard medical treatments that may only suppress or reduce symptoms.
Thanks to our body's ability to hold and store emotional traumas, we can access and release them through various bodywork practices, restoring liveliness and health.

Sometimes a massage will trigger a long buried memory of sexual abuse, sometimes energy work on the body—invisible and without touch—will allow a dam of emotions to break through and drain away. Tenderly praying with someone often brings cleansing tears.

The practice of point holding in Body Electronics bores in on "crystals" of hardened resistance that build up and block major channels of vitality.

Body Electronics teaches that meeting any life experience with less than open-hearted enthusiasm precipitates some amount of toxicity or hardening at a cellular level that eventually adds up to make a crystal, like drips of dissolved limestone creating a stalagmite.

During a table session with a nutritionally prepared "appointee," pressing on the skin above these crystals releases vivid memories of all kinds of physical and emotional trauma, as though the crystals held the memories like computer chips.

We re-experience in the **Present** moment what we once emotionally resisted on a scale ranging from going unconscious to going ballistic. Point holders learn and coach one another to relax and allow the painful incidents along with our resistance that generated the crystals to come to light.

If we are willing to endure the body memory and become **Present** to the formerly refused experience, we can then engage in the heroic (and thoroughly counter-cultural) work of loving the pain and healing the resulting physical damage.

Going back into one's physical, mental and emotional pain this way can be brutal but effective of miraculous cure.

It is possible, even natural, to be so in tune with our bodies, to be so aware of our state of health as to prevent illness or intuitively know the most appropriate course of cure.

We see this with animals who fast, rest, seek water, or chew greens when they are sick. Most modern humans lose this natural ability by numbing our systems with drugs and clogging them with unhealthy food. This can be undone.

As a very young child, my son was diagnosed with allergies to wheat, dairy, soy, sugar, cold air, dust, mold, penicillin, drugs, and artificial chemicals in the environment as well as his food.

After eliminating these as much as possible and building up his immune system with Chinese herbs, he began to thrive so amazingly well that he became a standout among his peers, especially in the arts, athletic ability, and physical grace.

Best of all, my son learned to connect the dots between what he put in his mouth and how he felt afterward—an innate ability most children don't have much chance to develop.

Though he long since began making his own food choices, he still feels and knows better than I do what the consequences are.

Eating more naturally will make it easier to be **Present** in your body. First, because the toxin load and resulting sluggishness will be less, but also because you will feel better and enjoy having a body more.

To practice embodied **Presence**, notice just how willing you are to be here in your body and what your relationship to your physical self has been over the years.

Can you be grateful for all the experiences your body has made possible for you?

We are given the wondrous gift to be mortal, to be a particular, specific work of art, a snowflake. It is a joy to be so honored to be **Present.**

Can you be willing to be more **Present** to sensory experience?

Notice again how you feel in your body now. Does anything still hurt? Can you be aware of your breathing, your pulse? What do you hear, see, taste, smell, feel?

Let go of the need to react or do anything about what you notice for a moment and just be with what comes into your senses from the environment around you.

Some workshop participants tell how they feel the **Grace** of **Presence** when riding their motorcycles. Whether roaring along in traffic when any wrong move could be life threatening, or thrilling to the wind on their faces and connection to the countryside unshielded by a box of metal and glass, their senses are fully alert and they feel alive.

Just to be is a blessing. Just to live is holy.
---Rabbi Abraham Heschel

Something wonderful happens when we choose to be fully **Present** for each other.

If we relax and let go of our self-focus and the internal streaming reactivity, being with another human is incredibly healing for both.

Try it on a loved one today and see for yourself. Take their hand. Look into their eyes and see into their soul as you listen to them.

Deep listening, without the need to agree or disagree, criticize, or buy into what is being said is powerful medicine.

Truly hearing someone is the mark of love, the mark of the body of Christ, the mark of being open, the mark of not at war: "I am here."

Around your fellow humans as you go about your day, practice simply being the eyes that see, ears that hear, fingertips that feel.

Receive into your awareness everything you can—without inner commentary—and then open to receive more.

When you are the awareness into which everything is a blessing coming in, you are also a blessing radiating out.

Do this when you are on the street, at the store, restaurant, and bank around your fellow humans who are usually invisible to you and you to them.

You will experience just how uplifting and sweet it is to connect for a moment with others in **Presence.**

The present moment is timeless. The ancient Greeks had a word for the timely, timeless, right moment: *kairos.*

It is art. It is also worship. Not the paradigm of worship as fall-on-your-face **Awe** in the presence of Transcendence, but being **Present** to the still, small voice of silence.

Aligned in the present moment, in the *kairos,* we somehow know just what to do without calculation or dither. Often there is no action required, just being.

Can you remember when you were there, fully **Present**? Can you be there now?

It is actually easier to be **Present** than absent, lost in thoughts or feelings about the past even if that has become an ingrained habit of mind.

It is easier to be **Present** because *Present is the present* and the past is dead. You have to resuscitate it. You have to breathe into it. You have to drag it forward. You have to stand up the corpse of the past and pretend that it is truly here—all of which takes a great deal of your life energy.

Living in the **Present** is not denial of the past, for denial is a form of resistance and **Self Protection** that is also costly of your life force**.**

Rather, it is giving each moment permission to be new, to be itself what it is, without imposing bias or judgment based on memories of past experience.

We can make being present easier or harder for each other. If two or more people conspire to impose some past memory on Now, they will succeed relatively well and no one will be surprised that nothing much changes.

But if one party to the interaction does not join the conspiracy of biasing the **Present** from past memory, even if their dance partner insists on bringing their memory to bear on today, they will have only half the power to do this than they would have with the other's collusion.

And so no matter what they do, it is to some degree a new and never before seen and completely different situation.

If both conspire to be **Present**, however, then what is **Present** is what is **Present** without regard to anything else. It can then be quite new and different from what was. And that is easier, and certainly more wonderful than conspiring together to recycle the past.

Try this out today and prove to yourself that living in the **Present** is both easier and more wonderful than dragging the past around or worrying about a nonexistent future.

****

What foods might enhance our awareness of the **Present** moment?

Paradoxically, in our mindless eating, fast food culture, *slow* foods might be a good spiritual practice for **Presence**.

Really slow raw foods might need to be sprouted or dehydrated over several days before they are ready to eat. Patience is one of the exquisite "fruits" of the Holy Spirit and the virtue of a saint.

Sprouting

There are two basic methods—sprouting seeds in just water and sprouting them in water for a few days and then planting them thickly in potting soil. The plants are then cut with a scissors or knife to use as microgreens or grasses. Whichever method you are using, sprouts are about the most alive food you can put in your mouth. I rely on sprouting much more in the winter when garden greens aren't as available.

<u>Sprouting in water</u>
Start with fresh organic seeds and soak in filtered water 2-4 hours if tiny seeds like alfalfa and clover, 4-8 hours for larger seeds such as sunflower and wheat berries. You don't need anything but a jar and a strainer with appropriate sized holes. I use nut milk bags, colanders and kitchen strainers. You can also purchase plastic screw caps in various sizes that fit quart canning jars.

After soaking, rinse and drain your seeds and set near the sink, so you will remember to rinse them 1-2 times a day. Lentils, mung beans, garbanzo and other dried beans, sunflower seeds, wheat, rye, kamut, and spelt are ready when their little root tails are showing, usually just a day or two. Flax, sesame, chia, buckwheat, amaranth, quinoa, pumpkin seeds, almonds, oats and wild rice are ready to use after they have been soaked and rinsed, though a day of sprouting will not hurt. Longer times at room temperature may cause mold to form, so drain your sprouted seeds well and put them in the refrigerator for up to a couple days if you are not using them right away.

Note: *mucilaginous seeds like chia and flax are usually just soaked and not rinsed before incorporating them into raw dishes.*

Alfalfa, broccoli, clover, radish, cress, onion, etc. are sprouted longer to green up. This may take up to a week. Be sure to keep rinsing and draining off the water at least once each day while they are growing, and put the sprout container in the sunlight. After they are sprouted sufficiently, they will keep refrigerated for about a week if they are neither soggy nor dry.

Microgreens

There are many seeds you can use for microgreens, but buckwheat, peas, and sunflower seed—with the hulls—along with wheat, kamut, spelt, and rye grass are the most common. You can purchase flats to hold the potting soil or just use any shallow large container such as the round drip trays for plants or old cafeteria trays as Ann Wigmore suggested.

Besides containers and a good organic potting soil, I go to the trouble of adding a big pinch of agricultural minerals to the planting mix, such as glacial rock dust, azomite, or sea solids. Your lusty young plants will take up all these minerals and chelate them for you and your body will greatly benefit.

Soak your seeds for the recommended time—not too long or you will drown them. Then drain them and cover your prepared soil in a solid layer 1 seed thick. Make sure the soil is moist, cover your container and keep in a warm place for a day or two to germinate. Then uncover, place in a window or outside if weather permits, and keep well watered but not soggy until your greens are ready to pick. 2-6 inches of height is the ideal for most plants. You can harvest what you need each day, but cut them all within a week or before they exhaust the soil and become pot bound. Slightly damp cut greens will stay fresh another day in a plastic bag in the fridge.

Dehydrating

Ah, the mainstay of raw gourmet, adding texture, shelf life, and increasing the types of dishes you can create! There is some sacrifice of enzymes in drying food, though, even if you control the temperature and keep it low enough to preserve the enzymes. So keep crackers, chips, nuts, and cookies around for snacks and to round out your meals, but make sure to drink extra water when you eat them and focus predominantly on fresh raw fruits and vegetables otherwise.

As far as equipment goes, you can get great results with the inexpensive round food dryers with a central hole for bottom heat or a pricier dehydrator with a side fan and multiple rectangular trays. I also have a solar dryer, but rarely find it useful in rainy Oregon where I live.

Dried Fruit Candy

It doesn't get much easier than putting fruit slices on the mesh sheets of your dehydrator and turning it on until they are chewy-dry enough to store in a jar in the cupboard. Drying concentrates the sugars, which act as a preservative. Here are some fruits that dry especially well:

cantaloupe slices
watermelon chunks—will shrink a lot and keep their color
persimmon slices
mango strips
apple slices
peach slices
plum halves
Asian pear/American pear slices
banana strips
pineapple bits
kiwi slices
cherries-pitted

Banana brittle

To keep this crisp, store in airtight container in the fridge. It's good chewy, though.

5 ripe bananas (with brown spots on skin)
1 c walnut pieces
cinnamon

Puree bananas in a food processor with the S blade. Pulse in walnuts, but leave bits. Pour onto Teflex or solid dehydrator sheet about 1/8" thick. Sprinkle with cinnamon and dry until crisp.

Simplest Banana Bread

Just 3 ingredients you probably have on hand. Delicious breakfast treat that keeps well.

6 very ripe bananas
½ c golden flax seed
1 t cinnamon

Puree bananas in a food processor with the S blade. Grind flax seeds in a coffee grinder or dry Vitamix and pulse in with the bananas and cinnamon until mixed. Spread on Teflex or solid dehydrator sheets and dry until they can be peeled off. Remove sheets and finish drying to a chew consistency on the mesh sheet. Cut and store in a covered container.

Cranberry Scones

Make these with your extra almond pulp. They are festive and deliciously soft.

2 c fresh or frozen almond pulp
½ c golden flax seed
2 apples or pears, chopped
2 c carrots, chopped
1 c fresh or frozen cranberries
½ c raisins
½ c walnuts, chopped, optional
2 T extra virgin coconut oil, warm enough to be at least somewhat soft
¼ c raw honey, pitted dates, agave, or coconut nectar raw sweetener
2 t cinnamon
1 t cardamom, ground
½ t unprocessed salt

Puree apples or pears with carrots in a food processor. Blend in coconut oil, cinnamon, salt and sweetener of choice. Pulse in almond pulp. Turn into a bow. Mix in cranberries , raisins, and walnuts, if using. Grind flax seeds in a coffee grinder or dry Vitamix, add to mixture and thoroughly hand mix. Shape into round patties about 5" in diameter and ½" thick. Pat onto dehydrator sheets. Score tops to make a star pattern with 6 triangles. Dry for a few hours until they can be lifted off the sheets to continue drying on the mesh until dry but still soft.

Spicy Yam Chips

There are two secrets to a good root vegetable chip. One is to slice the roots very thin. A mandoline works best for this, especially if you are making a lot. The other secret is to use a very light touch with the oil or your chips will be greasy.

2-3 yams
2 t extra virgin coconut oil
1 t unprocessed salt
1 t curry powder

Peel and slice yams just less than 2 mm thick. Toss with oil, salt and curry and arrange on mesh sheets to dry until crisp.

Simplest Kale Chips

2 bunches kale, washed and de-stemmed
1 t extra virgin olive oil
½ -1 t unprocessed salt

Toss kale with oil and salt, place on mesh dehydrator sheets and dry on low until crisp.

Kale Chips

Probably the tastiest way to ingest a lot of nutritious kale. For the last several years, some form of this delicacy has been showing up as a raw standard. Variations include tahini and teriyaki flavors, and just plain oil and salt.

2 large bunches kale
1 c cashews, soaked just one hour
1 red bell pepper, seeded and chopped or 1 large carrot or ½ c butternut squash
¼ c lemon juice
1 T Nama Shoyu or Coconut Aminos
1 t unprocessed salt
Optional: ½ c nutritional yeast, ½ jalapeno pepper

Wash, de-stem, and drain kale leaves. Tear or chop into rough pieces. Blend vegetables and spices until liquid. Drain cashews and blend into the vegetable liquid. Pour over leaves and toss until coated. Spread on mesh sheets and dry until crisp.

Spiced Nuts and Seeds

The basic recipe is to soak the nuts and seeds for a few hours first; rinse and drain. Then sprinkle on your chosen herbs and spices. Try these and then experiment:

Hulled sunflower seeds with curry powder
Pistachio nuts with chili powder, onion powder, salt
Walnuts with garam masala and Nama Shoyu or Coconut Aminos

Prize Winning Onion Sesame Crackers

This took first prize over tough competition at the annual Krazy Kracker Contest at our 2010 Raw and Living Spirit Retreat. They have that winning flavor and crunch that Abeba Wright, the Krazy Kracker Lady, demands. Our friend Donna Curtis agreed to share her recipe.

1 large sweet onion
1/4 c lemon juice (1-2 lemons)
1/2 c golden flax, ground
1 tsp. Himalayan crystal salt
1 c sprouted buckwheat (soak 20 minutes, rinse, sprout about 8-10 hours. Dehydrate overnight)
1/2 c tan sesame seeds
1/2 c black sesame seeds (stir in)

1- Soak buckwheat 20 minutes, rinse well. Sprout 8 hours or so. Dehydrate 105 degrees, overnight.
2- Chop one onion in food processor.
3- Add 1 tsp. salt and ¼ cup freshly squeezed lemon juice. Process.
4- Grind ½ cup golden flax well. Add and process.
5- Add 1 cup sprouted, dehydrated buckwheat and ½ cup tan sesame seeds. Process just until mixed (don't puree the buckwheat entirely or you'll change the texture of the final cracker)
6- Pour onto one Teflex dehydrator sheet. Add and fold-in black sesame seeds. Spread evenly over sheet. Use a hard spatula to shape edges and smooth the top. Score crackers into desired size and shape.
7- Dehydrate at about 105 F for 3-4 hours on Teflex sheets. Flip onto mesh sheets to ensure proper drying. Total dehydrating time will be 12 to 16 hours.
*Note-Black sesame seeds add a little extra flavor and enhance appearance. But stir in, don't process or they turn crackers an unappealing gray color.

Minh's Marinated Tomatoes

Minh Skurow, of the dynamic duo Ronnie and Minh, first shared her version of these in wonderful stuffed zucchini rolls she made for the Raw and Living Spirit Retreat one year. Now they are essential to my lasagna recipe, as well as my favorite topping for cashew-hemp cheese. That is, if I don't eat them all just scooping them off the dehydrator trays. Partially dehydrating really perks up the tomato flavor while retaining the softness.

10 medium to large tomatoes; Romas work best as they have less juice.
2 T extra virgin olive oil
2 T Italian seasoning with garlic
1 t unprocessed salt

Slice tomatoes in evenly about ¼" thick and place in large nonmetallic bowl. Add remaining ingredients and toss gently until tomato slices are coated. Lift slices from liquid with a slotted spoon on to mesh dehydrator sheets and dry for a few hours to overnight. Remove from sheets while still soft and flexible and store in fridge until needed.

Puris

This simple flax bread can be eaten plain or used for a pizza platform or a sandwich wrap. Our friend Shanti Moon of Nourishing Elements showed us how to make them. Take the puris out of the dehydrator when they are dry but still flexible.

1 c golden flax seed
2 dates
1 T coconut oil
2 c filtered water
½ t unprocessed salt

Soak flax in the water for 14- hours. Blend with other ingredients in a Vitamix until smooth and spread out onto Teflex sheets in thin pancakes to dehydrate until dry but still pliable.

Sweet Onion Bread

This is my take on Matt Amsden's original recipe in RawVolution. Just about everyone loves it as a platform for an avocado sandwich, seed cheese pizza, or just plain. We make this in massive amounts and even ordered a special 2 mm slicer blade for our Cuisinart to speed up the process.

12 large sweet onions
½ c Nama Shoyu, Coconut Aminos, or 4 T miso diluted in ½ c water
2 c flax seed (you may substitute 1 c chia for 1 cup of the flax)
2 c hulled sunflower seed (you may substitute 1 c quinoa for 1 c of the sunflower)

Slice the onions as thin as possible with a knife, mandoline, or 2 mm food processor blade. Place in a large non-metallic bowl. Stir in chosen marinade, cover and let sit for 2 hours to overnight, stirring occasionally. Just before using, grind seeds into flour in a dry Vitamix or other grinder. Mix thoroughly by hand. Pat on to a solid dehydrator sheet ¼" thick.

Quick Drying technique:
Lay a mesh covered tray on top of the onion bread dough, flip over, and peel off the solid sheet to allow the bread to dry more quickly on the mesh tray. When half dry, cut into pieces with clean kitchen shears and continue drying until done but still a bit flexible.

Nori Snacks

*One of the ways to make sea vegetables taste good. Nice with a warm bowl of **Marvelous Miso Soup** (page 103) and a salad.*

2 c hulled sunflower seeds, soaked and sprouted 1 day (will expand about double after soaking)
2 cloves garlic, minced
¼ c Nama Shoyu or Coconut Aminos
8 sheets untoasted Nori

Rinse sunflower seeds in a colander and place in food processor with the garlic and liquid ingredient. Pulse until blended into a rough paste. With dry hands, cut nori sheets into 4 pieces. Place 1 T paste in a strip along the bottom of each small sheet and roll up. You can seal the flap with a finger wet in a bowl of water. Continue making rolls until all of the paste is used up. Arrange rolls on a mesh dehydrator sheet and dry on low until done, about 6 hours.

Pizza Crust Cracker

One of the many variations we've used for pizzas at Sunday Supper. This makes use of chewy sprouted kamut.

1 c kamut, soaked and sprouted for 2 days (will expand after soaking to about 2 c)
1 c hulled buckwheat, soaked and sprouted for 1-2 days (will expand in bulk after soaking)
1 c lentils, soaked and sprouted for 2 days (about doubles in bulk after sprouting)
1 c flax seed
¼ c extra virgin olive oil
1 t unprocessed salt
filtered water

Grind flax seed in dry Vitamix or coffee grinder. Rinse sprouts, combine in blender with oil, salt and water to cover. Blend until smooth. Blend in ground flax. Mixture will thicken quickly. Spread on solid dehydrator sheets about 1/8" thick for crackers or ¼" thick for pizza crust. Dehydrate until almost dry but still flexible.

Onion Bread, Cranberry Scones, Yam Chips, Puris, Alfalfa and Sunflower Sprouts

Chapter 8

Love

The greatest of these is love.--1 Corinthians 13

From **Presence** we notice we are in **Love.**

From wherever we are, it is always a small step to **Love.** For **Love** is our truth and our true nature.

Love is our beginning and our end. **Love** is all-encompassing—both a gift and a fruit of the Holy Spirit.

It is the lodestar and the sum total of the **Compass of Grace.**

The defining quality of **Love** is union. It is the *unum* of our *pluribus*.

When we observe a separation, then realize that the meaning we have created out of our observation is imaginary, and choose to erase the imaginary meaning, we have **Love.**

Love is one word for the foundation of the created universe. As the foundation, or what the house sits on, it is also a word for another undefinable word, which in English is God.

God is love.--1 John 4:8

We have all experienced *conditional* love.

Can you remember how that feels?

Much cultural training is to do something, earn something, deserve something to be worthy of love.

Once love becomes a commodity, it is a limited good to fight over, to win, to lose.

In the **Compass of Getting Along**, everything we see as "love" is basically subject-object, whether it be the much desired *eros,* or *philos*, the love of like kind.

Full **Love** is wider than the embrace of what we want or like or identify with.

Full, Godlike, unconditional **Love**, is compassion—or what the New Testament calls *agape*—beyond passion, or even the tribal love of *philos*.

All-encompassing **Love** is powerful enough to overcome every flavor of separation and self protection.

The opposite of **Love** is hate, which leads to murder and annihilation. Ever notice how quickly a caring, seemingly loving relationship can turn to resentment and hatred?

The eyes of **Love** see only Oneness, see that all hate is self-hate, all murder, self-murder.

Jesus, who embodied *agape-love,* loved his enemies and fearlessly "descended into hell" to save the lost.

Love is patient and kind, never jealous or boastful or arrogant or rude. It does not insist on its own way; is not irritable or resentful; does not keep track of wrongdoing, but rejoices in the truth. Love bears all things, believes all things, hopes all things, endures all things. Love never ends.
--1 Corinthians 13

When did you ever feel that kind of **Love**?

Where were you and what was happening when it touched your heart?

Bring the memories forward into the ever-present now and let yourself see, hear, smell, taste, touch, feel it—all around, up, down, and sideways. Is anyone there with you, sharing the bliss of your wide open heart?

Often it may be a child. Hold yourself as a young child in the light of this **Love**.

Make it more. Remember your deep truth of **Love.**

Many people don't like the word "religion," but its root meaning is *re-ligare,* "to rejoin, " which is the impulse of **Love** as we are defining it. In embodied spirituality and true religion, **Love** is neither a glittering generality, nor a wished-for elusive butterfly, but manifests where we live.

And since mostly where we live is either in the world of **Self Protection** or **Getting Along**, manifesting gracious **Love** changes the world.

Circle gatherings at Christ the Healer are quite diverse. We seem to attract personalities who are strongly attached to belief systems on many subjects, but especially food and religion.

Over the years we have learned to create an open and accepting space for people to share their perspectives on the topic at hand.
Mostly we find that people welcome, accept, and even enjoy the diversity of points of view expressed.

Occasionally the group is challenged when someone—who often turns out to be an angel visiting us unawares—asserts a religiously held opinion that seems exclusive and judgmental.

Often it is an evangelical Christian speaking their truth, though sometimes we hear words from the fringes of consensual reality that can stop the conversation as well.

Last time this happened, we were talking about how we might love our neighbors. On a Christmas visit, the mother of one of our Sunday Supper chefs proclaimed that you could only love if you had Jesus in your heart first.

The happy flow of discussion in the circle instantly shut down into a tense silence.

What's a pastor whose career has been reaching out to religiously-averse spiritual seekers to do?

Breathe, go into the grace of **Acceptance**, and wait to see what happens.

What happened was a newer person who had previously never spoken in the circle spluttered that as someone who had left narrow-minded Christianity far behind for an earth based spirituality, she had to disagree.

The tension grew. Then a young friend of the chef (who was by now trying to melt into the back wall) uttered inspired words to the effect that, "We all agree that God is **Love.** That means **Love** is God. If we agree on that, we have more in common than it may seem."

Whew, it worked! Nobody darted for cover. The circle held the tension by expanding around it, not cutting anyone out.

Love and I conspired to win
We drew a circle that took them in

For me, the greatest human manifestation of God's **Love** known to history is Christ, who was in Jesus.

But I see how Christ can also be in each of us, as Buddhists have recognized with the term "Christ mind" and Hindus with "Christ Consciousness."

I say Christ is the universal **Love** of God made manifest. Jesus, who knew himself as one with God, constantly invited and encouraged everyone to follow him and be as he is.

There is no need or excuse for any exclusiveness in Christian dogma or practice. We are *commanded* to **Love**. Fully.
Love the Lord your God with all your heart, with all your soul, with all your mind, and with all your strength....Love your neighbor as yourself. There is no commandment greater than these.
                                                    --Mark 12:28-31

Love your neighbor as yourself.

You can make an interesting practice of taking that quite literally. Imagine that each neighbor you encounter is actually you, not a separate reality.

This really changes how we look at the people on the street, in the news, the store, in our families, at work and play. Say to yourself as you look at them, "I am another you."

What happens when you deeply feel that to be true? A whole lot of harmony reigns where it was missing before.

For practice, Thomas and I made "I am another you" our mantra for awhile and coined this contraction of the phrase to sign our emails: Iyou.

There is a related practice called *ho'oponopono,* a modern application of a traditional Hawaiian ritual of group reconciliation.

It involves identifying with your threatening or even criminal neighbor so much that you forgive *yourself* for whatever they are perceived to be guilty of.

Here's a prayer I created and still use to climb out of **Self Protection** when I'm stuck seeing bad guys.

> *I love you*
> *I am you*
> *I forgive this*
> *I accept forgiveness and healing*
> *Thank you.*

Do you aspire to an expanded awareness of **Love**? Here are some wise words I was given once when I asked for an exercise to **Love** more fully:

Notice how every particle in what you experience as creation, down to the very smallest, which as you know is not a particle at all, is love.

And notice how love masks itself by interfering with love.

Notice the interference patterns that you label as non-love.

Notice how the joy of unity is present in a dust mote that floats in the air, separated from all other dust motes, and how it moves upon molecules of other types, and finally, no matter how light, settling upon dust motes of the past to form the earth.

How the separation and reunion of love is the only story.

The love of dust motes, the love of grains of sand, the love of chemical interaction, the love of gravitation, the love of humans who wish to rub upon each other, the love of humans who stand in circles—it is the same love.

It is unity.

There is oneness and there is the dispersal of oneness. And the re-aggregation of oneness.

All other distinctions are the descriptions of the game any lover is playing.

Notice how a chair loves you. Every molecule in this aggregation has allowed itself to be molded into a caress for your comfort.

Every irritating fool has allowed himself or herself to be molded into a mirror for your enhancement. There is nothing that does not love you.

Is anyone having trouble with all this talk of **Love?** At the root of our wounded psychology may be a fear of being discovered as undeserving of **Love.**

This can be hidden behind a belligerence that says, "I don't deserve, I have never deserved, there is no **Love** for me. And since there is no **Love,** I will stop trying to deserve it."

There is **Love.** We are fully loved for no reason. We never had to do anything to deserve **Love,** and couldn't possibly begin to. God, who is the loving foundation of the universe, loves us.

Here's how to prove it to yourself: Give up the goose chase of looking to be loved, to have **Love,** and instead ask, "How can I *give* **Love**?"

You will discover that you do have **Love** because you have some to give.

When we stop running after what we think is love and instead trust the **Love** that is shown in everything in the universe loving us if we will only notice, it is easy to *be* **Love,** to experience ourselves as **Love.**

When one is **Love,** only **Love,** one is like a sun radiating. There is no loss. The sun is not taking chunks of sun-ness and merely giving, the sun is **Love.**

If there are two suns and they radiate on each other, then there is **Love** loving **Love.** In the psychology of getting, when one looks for love to be given—a losing game, because we have all the **Love** we need by *being* **Love**—one does not radiate but engages in give and take.
The gracious can enjoy being **Love** even if they are engaged in relationships with conditionally loving or unlovely others.

Even a sun radiating on an ice ball that refuses to melt is no less a radiant sun. There is no condition of reciprocation.

The one who is **Love** is perfectly filled with **Joy** because that one is in **Love** with everything in every place. "I am not engaged in commerce, I simply am." And that is fulfilling.

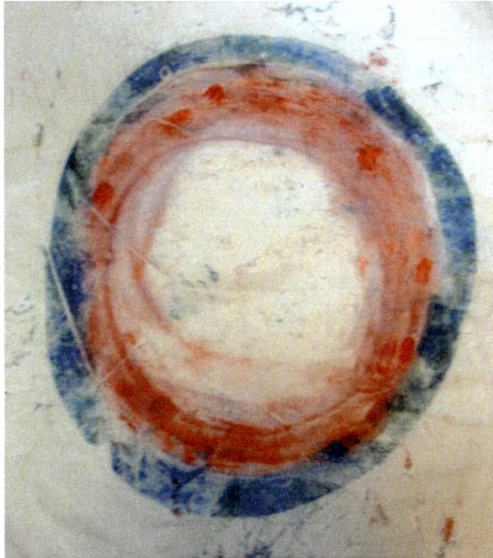

One
Dana Kelly Sweet

There are basically two paths to greater wholeness and they both involve **Love.**

We can either learn to discipline our psychology, move away and beyond our limited view of ourselves and the world, as in the exercise above, or we can honestly face and embrace the pain and accumulated damage we have created in our human operating systems by our resistance to the fullness of **Love**, and witness it implode.

Since 1995 I have been subjecting myself to the latter method in our Body Electronics practice because so far I have been a slow learner in bringing my whole mind-body-emotional human operating system into alignment with the higher truth of Oneness that I intellectually and in my heart espouse.

With Body Electronics, I can track any changes in consciousness, or *metanoias,* in my body's healing and renewal.

Since I participate in a weekly BE group and have been "on the table" many, many times, I have a certain confidence in my ability to handle what might come up in a session.

Yet not long ago, something surfaced that was safely buried beneath layers denial for all these years. As I lay on my face with seven friends pressing into painful hot spots, the first thing I became aware of—in a very physical way—was how often I was sick I as a child. The misery of it, now a full body memory, was so bad I wanted to die. I saw myself learning as a small child to escape my body's pain by suppressing awareness of how awful I felt.

Fast forward to an adult memory of my first marriage with that same sick feeling. Only this time the excruciating illness was associated with intense resentment I was experiencing in a memory of my ex.

The feeling was so ugly and repulsive to me and my idea of myself as a good person that I automatically engaged the skills honed in childhood to completely occlude any awareness of it.

Uncovering that pus pocket 20 years later felt impossibly painful. Internally in agony, I forgot all my skills of loving the pain and called out for help.

Grace answered when one of my friends responded and reminded me how we often meditated together, offering to do it again with me then and there.

Within ten minutes, her **Love** and our shared practice pushed me through the table work to an ecstatic finish.

And at the end, I could even feel my ex-husband in my heart for the first time in many years.

The top note of what BE calls the "Emotional Tone Scale" is enthusiasm.

Enthusiasm, *en-theos,* literally means being filled with God, being **Love,** being **Grace.**

Enthusiasm is our God-given natural state.

Yet here on earth, bound in a body equipped with a human operating system, we quickly encounter more overwhelming sensation and pain than we are ready to encompass with **Love**.

Stopped from enthusiasm at the pain barrier, we begin our tumble down the tone scale. Creating and reinforcing habitual resistance to pain, we become less alive by degrees until we are officially pronounced dead.

The good news is that we can either become enlightened—realize and live life knowing that whole drama is not our essential truth—and/or we can engage loving practices to reverse engineer the damage to our human operating systems.

Our beautiful bodies can take us home to **Love.**

We humans can become discouraged and give up, or look for salvation only after death. Even those of us who believe in the return of Christ or a new age may expect it only as an apocalypse after massively destructive tribulation.

There is another alternative.

Many say they believe in the risen Christ. That means Christ as **Love** is present, active, available to all who seek or ask.

Love and **Grace** are universal and open to all without qualification or condition.

God can be found within and without and most wonderfully, manifested in embodied humanness, laboring silently to be "born in us today" as the carol sings.

This is a "second coming" of Christ we don't have to wait for, let alone dread.

"How do you get to Carnegie Hall? Practice, practice, practice," the old joke goes.

How do you get to the kin-dom of heaven? There is no getting, we are already immersed in it. It is **Grace** and truth.

In bodies we play the games of "let's pretend we are separate" and then get lost in our games.

Using the **Triple Compass Map** and the **Compass of Grace**, we can attune to our truth and find   our way home again.

It can happen now.

It might take a little practice.

****

If **Love** is about coming together, not apart, then **Love** food means a community table. CtH UCC has fed crowds for years in festivals, retreats, potlucks, parties, special events, and since 2006, our weekly catered raw gourmet Sunday Supper.

Feeding a crowd is always a special challenge, more so when you are making multiple dishes from scratch with fresh ingredients. Our retreat and event chefs plan to spend all day in the kitchen with volunteers to turn out their raw gourmet feasts. Their work is their joy, truly a labor of **Love.**

And thankfully, there are no burnt or greasy pans to wash afterward! Owner-Chefs Lillian Butler and Eddie Robinson of the Raw Soul Restaurant in Manhattan have graced the Raw and Living Spirit Retreat a number of times and we always ask them to make their New York Cheesecake when they come.

One year I went to the kitchen in the morning to see what help they needed for their dinner for 150 that night. Eddie was just putting the finishing touches on 15 huckleberry topped cheesecakes.

Astounded, I learned that he'd gotten off the plane, gone into the kitchen, put on his hat and apron and worked through the night, squeezing a case of lemons and blending pounds of cashews all by himself. Then with Lillian and our volunteers, spent the rest of the day preparing the dinner.

When the diners were let into the candlelit dining room, they were delighted to see a huge slice of cheesecake dripping with the huckleberry sauce at each place.

Eddie came out and joked that in honor of the idea of food combining, they were serving the "fruit course" first. No one complained, and we have continued that particular tradition at the closing retreat banquet ever since.

After dinner, the indefatigable Eddie appeared on a panel called Raw Spirituality where he was asked what was the most important thing he had learned as a raw food chef. Eddie replied with an inscrutable smile: "Not to eat. Sometimes nutrition means more than food. I have not eaten since we arrived last night, but I am not hungry. I am filled and nourished by the **Love** of the food and the opportunity to prepare it for you."

Here are some of our favorite dishes for a communal table.

Chips and Dips

*Dips and pates are fast to make up fresh, when they taste the best. You can use any combination of nuts and seeds for a base, enhanced with vegetables, herbs, and spices. **Dill Dip,** below, is a favorite when fresh dill, an essential ingredient, is available. You can find the ingredients for **Sprouted Lentil Hummus** anytime. Each can be the center of a meal accessorized with crackers and a sliced veggie plate loaded with a combination of carrots, celery, jicama, turnip, daikon, broccoli, bell pepper, cauliflower, squash, snap peas, etc.*

Dill Dip/Pate

4 c sprouted sunflower seeds
2 c celery, chopped
1 bunch dill leaves chopped
1-2 cloves garlic
1/3 c lemon juice
¼ c extra virgin olive oil
1 T raw apple cider vinegar
1 pitted medjool date or equivalent raw sweetener
½-1 t unprocessed salt

Sprouted Lentil Hummus

In my first book I used garbanzo beans, which are more traditional. This version uses lentils, which are softer and blend more easily.

2 c lentils, soaked and sprouted for 2-3 days (will expand to about 4 c)
1 c unhulled sesame seeds, soaked for 2-4 hours, rinsed, and drained (or 1 c raw tahini)
½ c lemon juice
¼ c extra virgin olive oil
½ bunch celery, chopped
½ bunch parsley, chopped
2-4 cloves garlic
1 t unprocessed salt

Liquefy celery and parsley with the oil, lemon juice, garlic, and salt in a blender. Add sesame seeds or tahini and blend well. (Use a little water if needed to blend smooth.) Set aside half of the liquid and add half of the lentils. Blend until smooth, using the pusher. Put in a bowl. Add the remaining liquid and lentils, blend, and mix with the earlier batch. Adjust seasonings and serve.

Favorite Falafel

*Make extra hummus so you can use the leftover for this. Serve with **Fresh Tahini Dressing** and **Grain-Free Tabouli** (page 69)*

2 c prepared **Sprouted Lentil Hummus** (recipe above)
1 t ground cumin
1 t ground coriander
¼ c flax seed

Grind flax seed in a coffee grinder. Mix all ingredients together in a bowl. Let sit a few minutes to thicken, then using a small scoop, scoop out balls on to a mesh dehydrator sheet. Dry until crisp on the outside but slightly moist in the center, about 8 hours on low.

Pizza Party

The variations are endless. Here are a few ideas.

For the crust, use **Onion Bread, Puris, Pizza Crust Crackers,** or your own recipe. Spread with either **Cashew-Hemp Creamy Cheese,** (page 80) **Dill Dip,** (page 133) **Easy Pesto,** (recipe below) or just avocado mashed with a bit of miso. Toppings can be any combination of chopped vegetables, including tomato, bell pepper and onion, sprouts, pickles, **Fresh Marinara Sauce** (page 136) or minced herbs such as parsley, basil and cilantro. Try olives, **Minh's Marinated Tomatoes**, **Brazil Nut Rawmesan,** and sliced mushrooms marinated in a bit of Nama Shoyu or Coconut Aminos.

Revised Raw Lasagna

I'd been trying to perfect my original recipe which tended to get watery if you didn't eat it right away. Using Minh's Marinated Tomatoes in the layers and fresh tomatoes on top brought success. We make this on bakery half sheets (which still fit in most refrigerators) for a crowd, but this recipe fills a 9x12 glass baking pan. The fresh herbs take it to a new level.

2 c hulled sunflower seeds, soaked (will expand to about 4 c)
½ c fresh-squeezed lemon juice
1 clove garlic
½ t salt
1 T fresh thyme leaves
small sprig of fresh rosemary
small bunch of fresh basil
1 bunch fresh spinach
4 small or 2 medium zucchini or summer squash
2 cups **Minh's Marinated Tomatoes** (page 120)
¼ c **Brazil Nut Rawmesan** (page 71)
4 ripe red tomatoes
2 portabella mushrooms or 1 lb. crimini mushrooms
1 sweet onion
¼ c Nama Shoyu or Coconut Aminos

Preparation

First thinly slice the mushrooms and onion and place in a bowl, stirring in the Nama Shoyu or Coconut Aminos to marinate. Rinse and drain the sunflower seeds and process with the lemon juice, garlic, salt and herbs in a food processor or blender to a thick paste. Clean and pat dry spinach leaves. Slice zucchini very thin into lengthwise strips with a mandoline or vegetable peeler. Slice fresh tomatoes into 1/4" rounds. Have marinated tomatoes and **Brazil Nut Rawmesan** on hand and ready.

Assembly

Layer the bottom of the pan with half of the strips. Add a layer of spinach leaves. Carefully spread half of the sunflower seed cheese over all. Sprinkle the marinated tomatoes over that. Drain the mushrooms and onion and spread all of them over the tomatoes. Cover with the rest of the squash and then the rest of the seed cheese. Cover this with the fresh tomato slices and sprinkle the Brazil Nut Rawmesan on last.

Rainbow Vegetable Pasta Party

Spiralizers (one brand is called a Spirooli) can be found in kitchen specialty stores or ordered online. These neat hand-cranked tools turn vegetables such as zucchini, summer squash, sweet potatoes, butternut squash, beet, rutabaga, etc. into noodles. Alternately, you could finely julienne your vegetables with a knife or mandoline. Purchased raw kelp noodles are another choice.

Prepare several types of veggie pasta and place in separate serving bowls. Make the sauces below and put in bowls next to the pasta. You can also have some **Brazil Nut Rawmesan** and a bowl of naturally cured chopped olives available as toppings.

Fresh Marinara Sauce

6 ripe tomatoes, chopped
1 T extra virgin olive oil
1 c sun dried tomatoes
¼ c fresh basil, chopped
1 t Italian seasoning
unprocessed salt and fresh ground pepper to taste

Blend tomatoes and oil. Add dried tomatoes and let sit for about an hour to soften. Add the remaining ingredients and blend until smooth.

Easy Pesto

1 large bunch basil (4 oz. de-stemmed)
1 c walnuts or pine nuts
2 T extra virgin olive oil
1 T light miso
1-2 cloves garlic
unprocessed salt and fresh ground pepper to taste

Pulse nuts in a food processor until crumbly. Pulse in basil. Add rest of the ingredients and puree.

RawFredo Sauce

Macadamia nuts will be most fabulous in this recipe, but cashews and Brazils are just fine, too.

2 c macadamia, Brazil nuts, or cashews, in any combination, soaked for 1 hour
¼ c fresh-squeezed lemon juice
¼ c Nama Shoyu or Coconut Aminos
1 clove garlic
1 t unprocessed salt
fresh ground black pepper

Drain nuts, combine in blender with the other ingredients and blend until smooth.

Eggless Scramble

Serve this with a salad or roll up in a leaf wrap.

4 c soaked sunflower seeds, rinsed and drained
2 c celery, chopped
¼ c fresh parsley, chopped
1 large shallot, chopped
2 T extra virgin olive oil
1 T poultry seasoning
1 t cumin, ground
1 t turmeric, ground or 1 piece fresh root

Let Me Count the Ways Salad Bar

A tasty exercise in individual choice which results in uniquely beautiful plates.

Prepare a large bowl of mixed greens. Chop, grate and slice a variety of fresh salad vegetables and place in separate bowls on the serving table with the greens. Provide dressings and toppings (recipe suggestions in the **Joy** chapter), and pickles if you have some. Include a selection of chopped fruits to make a fruit salad, too.

Winter Spring Roll with Tamarind Dipping Sauce

Great anytime, but especially appreciated in winter when eating fresh seems more of an effort. Serves ten with a generous roll. When Clint made these on a cold Sunday Supper, we applauded warmly.

10 large collard greens, washed, tough stems cut out
5 large kale leaves, washed, de-stemmed and cut in 2
5 large green mustard leaves, washed and cut in 2
2 cups bean sprouts
1 large carrot cut into long matchsticks
1 mango cut into ribbons
1 red bell pepper sliced thin
1/2 c green onion, diced
1 c cilantro, chopped
1 c parsley, chopped
3/4 c basil, stems removed
3/4 c mint leaves, stems removed

Assemble wraps by first laying out the collard leaves and spreading with nut butter mixture, below. Then portion out and overlay the rest of the ingredients in the order given. Carefully roll up. Dip in Tamarind Sauce and eat!

Nut butter mixture
2 c raw almond butter (purchased or made by running dry almonds in a Cuisinart for 20 minutes or so until pasty)
1 cup finely chopped savoy cabbage
1/2 c agave syrup or coconut nectar
1 c fresh-squeezed lemon juice
2 T minced red chills (hot)
4 T fresh ginger, minced
2 T Nama Shoyu or Coconut Aminos

Pulse ingredients together in a food processor until mixed.

Tamarind dipping sauce
1 ½ c tamarind pulp (available in Asian sections as whole beans or pulp)
3-5 T agave syrup or coconut nectar
2 T Nama Shoyu
1 T extra virgin olive oil
Add filtered water as needed to blend to a sauce.

Taco Salad Dinner with Cashew Crème, Guacamole, and Salsa

Sunday Supper friend John Cleveland shared this menu with us recently. Yum!

Taco Salad

2 large heads romaine lettuce
2 c walnuts, soaked, rinsed, re-dried and chopped
2 T Nama Shoyu or Coconut Aminos
2 t cumin powder
1 t coriander powder
½ t unprocessed salt
½ t garlic powder, optional

Wash and pat dry the romaine leaves. Cut into bite sized pieces and place in large salad bowl. Mix the remaining ingredients by hand or pulse in a food processor and serve alongside the leaves with Guacamole, Salsa, and Cashew Crème.

Guacamole

4 ripe Hass avocados, peeled, seeded, and chopped
½ bunch cilantro, chopped
2 green onions, chopped
juice of 1 lemon
1 T raw apple cider vinegar
1 T Nama Shoyu or Coconut Aminos
½ jalapeno, seeded and chopped
½-1 t unprocessed salt

Blend everything together in a food processor or mash with a fork.

Salsa

3 ripe tomatoes, chopped
1 red or yellow bell pepper, diced
1 small red onion, diced
½ bunch cilantro, chopped
juice of 1 lime
1 T raw apple cider vinegar
½ – 1 t unprocessed salt

Stir everything together in a serving bowl.

Cashew Crème
1 c cashews, soaked for 1 hour (will expand a bit)
juice of 1 small lemon
1 T Coconut Aminos or Nama Shoyu
unprocessed salt to taste

Drain cashews. Place in blender with remaining ingredients and blend until smooth. Transfer to a squeeze bottle to serve.

Easter Basket Burritos

These beautiful "baskets" roll up into a big handful of new life.

1 red cabbage
4 c alfalfa sprouts
1 pint grape tomatoes
2 carrots, shredded
1 lb. baby spinach leaves
2 c prepared **Fresh Herb Ranch Dressing** (page 67)
edible flowers for garnish
kumquats, *optional*

Gently remove leaves from the cabbage, keeping them as whole as possible. Cover individual serving plates with baby spinach and nest the cabbage in the center. Toss sprouts with grated carrot and mound inside the cabbage leaves. Add a few chunks of avocado and 1-2 T of the dressing. Top with grape tomatoes, a kumquat if available, and edible flowers.

Warm Chili with Cashew Sour Cream

Angela discovered this recipe and introduced the improved version here at Sunday Supper. We always find someone licking the serving bowl when it's gone. It's rich— serve it with a big green salad.

2 c raw almonds, soaked 4-8 hours and rinsed
½ c chickpea miso
2 c carrots, chopped
2 T extra virgin olive oil
1 lb. mushrooms, chopped small
2 T raw apple cider vinegar
2 red, yellow or orange bell peppers, diced
2 cloves garlic
1 sweet onion, chopped fine
4 T fresh oregano
4 stalks celery, minced
2 t dried oregano
3 c sun dried tomatoes, soaked
2 T ground cumin
4 c filtered water, including tomato soak water
1-2 T chili powder, to taste
3 dates, pitted

Pulse almonds and carrots in a food processor until chunky. Place in large bowl with mushrooms, peppers, onion, and celery. Blend everything else until smooth and mix in with other ingredients. Serve at room temperature in warm bowls with a dollop of cashew sour cream.

Cashew Sour Cream
2 c raw cashews, soaked 1-2 hours
1 c filtered watercress
¼ c extra virgin olive oil
4 T lemon juice
1-2 t unprocessed salt to taste

Blend until smooth.

Bare Hands Picnic

This is an annual tradition at our Raw and Living Spirit Retreat, and consistently rates at the top of all the retreat meals in the evaluations. I usually teach an Intuitive Eating workshop right before, giving folks a chance to interact with different foods and notice how their bodies respond. Then we go outside to enjoy a glorious meal with no utensils. For dessert and entertainment, we challenge all comers to open the durians barehanded. Here's what you might find on the table:

raw ears of corn
snap peas
string beans
avocados
carrots
celery stalks
daikon radish
sweet peppers
broccoli
cauliflower
cherry tomatoes
greens for wraps
assorted pates
crackers
pickles
kim chi
sauerkraut
olives
cucumbers
sprouts
grapes
apples
pears
plums
nectarines
melons
strawberries
blueberries
cherries
figs
durian

Avocados On The Half Shell with Cucumber Mignonette Sauce

Sounds fancy, but it's easy to prepare. Serve on a bed of mixed greens.

4 large ripe Hass avocados
2 c **Dill Dip** (page 131) or **Eggless Scramble** (page 137)

Wash and pat dry avocados. Cut in half. Remove pits but not peel. Using an ice cream scoop, place a scoop of chosen pate where the pit was. Drizzle with Mignonette Sauce, below.

Cucumber Mignonette Sauce
1 c raw apple cider vinegar
1 shallot, minced
1" piece fresh ginger, grated
1 English cucumber, chopped
1 small handful cilantro, chopped
unprocessed salt and fresh ground black pepper to taste

Pulse together in a food processor until vegetables are minced. If your vinegar tastes too strong, add more cucumber or dilute with filtered water.

Easter Basket Burritos
Afterward

Practicing the Compass of Grace Where you Live

May we be blessed with Vitality
May we be blessed with Value
May we be blessed with Peace
--CtH Notebook of Words

Understanding the basic **Triple Compass Map** of the **Compass Way** is not difficult. The three areas of human experience it encompasses have been observed and described many times in many ways.

What we are calling **Grace, Getting Along,** and **Self Protection,** Jesus called "Heaven", "This World", and "Hell." You may call them something else.

With this simple map in mind, we never need be lost again in the otherwise confusing and changing territory of life and relationships. By reading this book or taking an introductory workshop, you will have learned to notice how each state feels in your own body as it out- pictures for you the expansion and relaxation of **Grace**, the focused tension of **Getting Along**, and the painful contraction of **Self Protection.**

Should you have any doubt at all as to where your consciousness is oriented in any given moment, those around you can tell you instantly.

Ideally, you will wish to share the **Compass Way** with your family and community. They will benefit personally, and you can enroll them to help your practice. Giving them permission to reflect back to you their perceptions of where you are coming from on the map will help your self-awareness grow. On the Compass of Grace website, www.compassofgrace.com you can join a group and find many more resources to support your growth in embodied grace.

Remember that the best use of wider self-awareness is wider self forgiveness.

When a fall from **Grace** is first acknowledged and then forgiven, self correction follows without an internal struggle.

Getting up again after such a stumble can be just this easy:

"Oh, I am fallen in the mud!" (self-awareness)

"Oh, I am muddy, I will have to wash, but I am OK. I forgive, I love me just as I am, lying in the mud." (self forgiveness)
"I stand up, I step away from the muddy puddle, I wash what needs washing. I move on down the road—until next time I trip!" (self correction)

There is no need to feel awful. To lie in the mud bewailing how poorly I have performed compounds the poorness. There is the need, rather, to do all three steps and be on the road again.

Living the **Compass Way** is something like being a guided missile. Guided missiles are called guided because over distance, they stray off course and need continual small course corrections. With these, they reach their aim, even after spending most of their trajectories out of line.

With self-awareness, self forgiveness, and self correction, we can continually choose and re-choose as we move through life. No blame, no shame, no burdening ourselves with guilt. No adding to the damage, but cleaning it up and moving on. No cursing the darkness, but rather lighting a candle.

Another way this wisdom has been given is to "Love what is." Not necessarily to like or approve of it, but to accept, be grateful, joyful, even, with what you've got.

What is loved, changes. What is resisted only gets more so, as objects pushing against one another actually hold each other up like an A-frame roof or two opponents locked in struggle.

When I hate something, I have what I have, plus hate. When I **Love** something, I have what I have plus **Love**. Which is better?

The **Compass Way** is simple, but not necessarily easy. As you practice, you will cultivate the habit of to bless and not to curse life as troubles arise. This will grow. You are aiming to be your best Self all of the time.

You are living the **Compass Way** when you open your eyes in the morning or close them at night and remember how it feels to be **Acceptance, Gratitude, Joy, Inspiration, Awe, Peace, Presence and Love**.

When, as you go about your day, you notice that you are fighting or stressing in painful **Self Protection** or fear-driven **Getting Along** and then forgive yourself.

What trips us up is that bind we are in. Our bodies and our minds have been formed in a consciousness of separation right down to the cells themselves, which at the most element level are simply membranes enclosing and defending an individual space inside of Unity.

And yet, with the **Compass Way** upgrade of our human operating system, we can actually bring an expanded consciousness of Unity right into the experience and perceptions otherwise defined and limited by our dualistically informed bodies.

This is accomplished when we identify with our essence and not the constrained, time-bound product of our sensory inputs, memory, habits, emotional reactivity, thinking, and culture which we might call our personality or small self.

With the self understanding and awareness gained through the **Compass Way** and by engaging practices that build our fluency in shifting to states of embodied **Grace**, we can truly reverse the vicious cycles of **Self Protecting** attack and defense built into our cells, and the endless and ultimately self defeating striving to **Get Along** ingrained into our psychological processing.

The remarkable adaptability of our own bodies as well as our inborn human potential for **Grace** allow us to replace the vicious cycles with "virtue cycles" we can create and pattern into our physiology and psychology. *Change your mind, change your brain.*

Here is a simple example of how you might use your practice of the **Compass of Grace** to create a "virtue cycle." First comes the choice. You might begin with a decision to serve another person in some way. This itself is an act of **Love**. You notice that you feel good when you give of yourself; then enhance and revel in the feeling as it grows into something that might be recognizable as delight or **Joy.** Acknowledging that **Joy** brings a sense of **Peace** or **Gratitude** about one's own situation. And that spreads to a feeling of more aliveness and vitality, the **Grace** of **Presence**.

Grace can't be contained, for it encompasses everything. From a perspective of duality, though, we have to expand our consciousness to be aware of what is truly all around us. When we choose to open and allow **Grace** in, even in some measure, we find that **Grace** never pools, but spreads—forever, inexorably, inviting us to lose our limited self-identification and embody the wonder of being both in this world yet not limited to it.

In my religious language this is consummation is called atonement; literally, "at-one-ment" or becoming whole. Healing is another word for becoming whole, as is salvation. Whatever you call it, to be Alive in **Grace** is the fulfillment of living, the constant great embrace of "Welcome Home!"

Go in Peace, Live in Grace
Trust in the arms that will hold you
Go in Peace, Live in Grace
Trust God's Love
---Billy Crockett "Bread for the Journey"

The Peace of Christ,
Love of God,
and Inspiration of the Holy Spirit
be with you now and always

Index of Recipes

About Gabrielle and Thomas Chavez

Rev. Gabrielle Chavez is the author of <u>The Raw Food Gourmet</u>, co-founder of The Raw and Living Spirit Retreat, and co-convenor of Christ the Healer UCC, the creative spiritual community where she and her husband Thomas originally developed the **Compass Way** and the **Compass of Grace.** The **Compass Way**, with its accompanying practice, amounts to a profoundly accessible reorientation of one's life and relationships to a higher level of expression.

After adopting a raw food lifestyle in 2001 to sustain her energetic organizational output, Gabrielle began incorporating her knowledge of plants into unique and beautiful raw gourmet dishes. An enthusiastic plant person since childhood, she cultivated her intuitive gardening skills with Machaelle Small Wright of Perelandra in Virginia and at the Findhorn Garden in Scotland. Gabrielle is "friends" with thousands of edible plants and flowers, both wild and cultivated, and shares her knowledge in Intuitive Eating workshops and Wild Food Walks.

Thomas C. Chavez is the author of <u>Body Electronics: Vital Steps for Physical Regeneration</u> published by North Atlantic Books, and <u>The Book of Life as we Live It</u> published by CoG Productions. He is a teacher, learner, and practitioner of a full spectrum healing lifestyle from food, body work, relationships and politics to energy work that leaps beyond the current bounds of his clients' imaginations. Thomas sees all these things as an integrated wholeness he calls prayer.

Gabrielle and Thomas reside at Grace Garden in Oregon City, Oregon, an urban permaculture homestead and informal community healing haven.

Made in the USA
San Bernardino, CA
26 December 2014